# Loving and Leaving
# a Church

# Loving and Leaving a Church

*A Pastor's Journey*

BARBARA MELOSH

WJK WESTMINSTER
JOHN KNOX PRESS
LOUISVILLE • KENTUCKY

*First edition*
Published by Westminster John Knox Press
Louisville, Kentucky

18 19 20 21 22 23 24 25 26 27—10 9 8 7 6 5 4 3 2 1

*Book design by Drew Stevens*
*Cover design by Marc Whitaker / MTWdesign.net*

**Library of Congress Cataloging-in-Publication Data**

Names: Melosh, Barbara, author.
Title: Loving and leaving a church : a pastor's journey / Barbara Melosh.
Description: First edition. | Louisville, Kentucky : Westminster John Knox Press, 2018. |
Identifiers: LCCN 2018006313 (print) | LCCN 2018023635 (ebook) | ISBN 9781611648386 (ebk.) | ISBN 9780664264345 (pbk. : alk. paper)
Subjects: LCSH: Melosh, Barbara. | Women clergy--Maryland--Baltimore--Biography.
Classification: LCC BR1725.M367 (ebook) | LCC BR1725.M367 A3 2018 (print) | DDC 284.1092 [B] --dc23
LC record available at https://lccn.loc.gov/2018006313

Most Westminster John Knox Press books are available at special quantity discounts when purchased in bulk by corporations, organizations, and special-interest groups. For more information, please e-mail SpecialSales@wjkbooks.com.

# CONTENTS

# INTRODUCTION

This is a story of saints and sinners—according to Luther, that's what we all are—and the story of Saints and Sinners, the small, blue-collar congregation in Baltimore where I learned how to be a pastor. When I arrived, they had been in decline for forty years, living off a dwindling legacy. When I left, the congregation was smaller still, and still struggling. So this isn't a success story—at least not a conventional one—but it's the story of many congregations today.

I went there aspiring to change them.

I knew better; really I did. But I fell for it anyway, fell hard for my own fantasies of rescue. I would be the one who would turn them around, reversing decades of decline. Like Pollyanna in the old movie, I'd roll up my sleeves and sweep away the dust of stale habit. I'd scrub the begrimed windows and hang prisms in them, so the sun would scatter sparks of light and color over the worn floors.

Instead, they changed me.

Long-suffering to a fault, they taught me patience. Unimpressed by my education and my credentials, they schooled me in humility. They drove me crazy and made me laugh. They moved me to tears and, some days, bored me to tears. They resented me and ignored me, tested and suffered me, accepted and loved me.

They called me "pastor," and among them, I became one.

As their pastor, I had a place in a community to which I otherwise did not belong. Compared to them, I was a rolling stone, roving from place to place to take advantage of educational opportunity or professional advancement. They stayed in place, deeply rooted in the neighborhood around the church and enmeshed in extended family. My membership in their tribe was provisional — by vocation, not birthright. The people of Saints and Sinners regarded me as the alien I was, and they trusted me anyway.

I baptized their children, witnessed their marriage promises, visited them in hospitals and nursing homes, gathered with them at funeral homes, and stood with them at the open graves of our beloved dead. With them I shared the push and tug of life together, with its misunderstandings and petty grievances and well-nourished grudges. I stood with them in the river of their pain and joy, with its undertow of unspoken resentment and anger and its deep currents of betrayal and grief, love and loyalty. We hurt one another and forgave one another and learned to love one another.

Yes, I devised to change them. I searched tirelessly for the latest church-growth program, glittering with promises of transformation. I visited these schemes upon the Saints with a zeal that left them bemused. I cajoled and encouraged, exhorted and hectored. Sometimes, I managed to convince a few people to follow the charge into congregational renewal. A few times, we got some traction: new members, new projects, new energy. But then the setbacks would send us slipping back. An enthusiastic newcomer would move away; a new council would rise up in rebellion; we'd be blindsided by a leak in the roof or a cold winter that sent the oil bill soaring or saw yet another boiler failure. I held on, at first with grit and determination, and eventually with a tenacity fueled by pride and delusion.

On the face of it, Saints and Sinners was a place where almost nothing seemed to happen. It seemed that way to me, sometimes. I writhed with frustration at the glacial pace of congregational life. I mounted campaign after campaign: leadership training, congregational renewal, transformational ministry. Most of them met a slow but certain death, dispatched by the congregation's vast indifference. Once in a while, something hit a nerve, and only then would the slumbering assembly rise as one to banish the threat of change.

The Saints loved their church, and they gave extravagantly of their time and their money and their very selves. But they loved the church as it was. Even more, they loved the church they had lost, the congregation of the early 1960s—the glory days. I burned to lead them into new life. They longed for restoration to their former glory, the bygone church whose image became ever more burnished with every passing year. They knew that church was gone forever, but they held on like death to what they had cherished. They understood what I denied, at first. Change is death.

I knew they were right about the costs of change—or I should have known. I had become a pastor because I was looking for a whole new life. To find it, I had to let go of the one I had. Along the way, I had wandered far from home. I had left behind the work I had known and loved, to become a beginner again. Then I left the community where I belonged, to become a stranger and sojourner with the Saints.

Call it a midlife crisis, or late midlife. Or call it the hound of heaven, in hot pursuit. Or the Holy Spirit, blowing me into a new life. Or call it surrender. Centuries before, Augustine, another wayward pilgrim, had written, "God, you have made us for yourself, and our hearts are restless till they find their rest in you."

By the late 1990s I had been a professor for nearly twenty years when a kind of restlessness began to overtake me: boredom with familiar routines, a growing impatience with my colleagues and my students and, most of all, myself. Then, under it all, an echoing emptiness, and a feeling I wasn't in the right place anymore. When I thought about keeping on for another fifteen or twenty years, I felt something like despair. But tenured positions are hard to come by, and people don't usually leave them. When they do, they don't usually become pastors. If you had told me years ago that this would happen to me, I would have laughed.

A pastor? I was hardly even a Christian.

I had grown up in church, but I'd left church and stayed out for some twenty years. "Unchurched." For months, sometimes years, I didn't even think about going to church. Yet something kept drawing me back—a longing I couldn't quite name or quell. I'd creep into the back of some church for a single Sunday, or several Sundays, for a month, a season, or even a year. And then I'd stop going for reasons I could name or for no reason at all, leaving church again.

I grew up in a Lutheran church; people like me are sometimes called "cradle Lutherans"—though I'm not sure I count as one, with those twenty years of wandering. I went to a dozen or so churches over those years, not all of them Lutheran. But when I joined a church again, it was a Lutheran church, and I became a Lutheran pastor. I think it was no accident that I returned to the place I'd begun. Lutheran theology challenges my intellect, fires my imagination, opens my heart. It fits me like a strand of DNA locking into its matching strand.

This is my story of Saints and Sinners, and I have tried to stay true to what I know—to tell my own story, and to recognize what I do not know and cannot know about the stories of others. Inevitably, though, my story involves and discloses the lives of others. I have tried to respect their stories by telling the truth as well as I know it. I include dialogue only when I wrote it down close to the time I heard or spoke it. In order to protect the privacy of others, I have sometimes changed identifying details, but I have not rearranged events, invented characters, or presented composites of people or places.

Pastors have the honor of sharing people's lives at profound and intimate moments. That trust is sustained by discretion and care, and pastors are bound by a code of confidentiality that does not end when a call ends. I've disguised some situations that appear here. In accounts where the events and participants are likely recognizable, I've talked with those involved. I use Amy's story, the most extended and intimate of these, with her family's gracious permission.

Most of the names in this book are pseudonyms. In this age of Internet search, these provide only light disguises, if any. But I have chosen this renaming as a way of reminding myself and readers that this story is shaped by the teller. Inevitably, others represented here may not agree with the way I have portrayed them, or myself, or the experiences we shared. From those who disagree with my account, I ask forbearance. From those I have hurt, I ask forgiveness.

Memory is a notorious trickster. Recent neuroscience confirms that which we knew all along: that we invent our stories as soon as we tell them, even to ourselves. Nonetheless, I have been formed as a writer by my first vocation as a historian, and I have tried hard to write an accurate account. As I found myself in the curious position of researching my own life, I relied on a variety of sources. I've mined volumes of journals, kept more or less continuously since I was nineteen years old. This kind of personal writing is itself shaped by selection and emotion, but it offers the advantage of a written record and reflection set down closer to the events. I've consulted years of datebooks that helped me reconstruct a timeline of events and that documented the rhythms and activities of my days.

Letters from friends and an important mentor, Thomas R. Swears, provided some insight into my own state of mind at different points. Since 1998, when we met at a ministry-formation event at Gettysburg, I've maintained a correspondence with Laura Lincoln. Until 2012 we wrote each another every month with few exceptions; her letters document our paths through ministry and reveal the struggles and texture of my years with the Saints. I've also consulted friends and relatives for their memories of events.

The paper trail left by candidacy and seminary work has helped me reconstruct other parts of this story. In particular, I've made use of the reflective writing taught in clinical pastoral education. The verbatim is a description of a pastoral encounter done close to the event, in which the writer is challenged to observe closely and record as fully and accurately as possible. Those accounts preserved the immediacy and intensity of that experience, and honed skills of observation and reflection that served me well as a pastor and as a writer.

Emotional truth is another matter. I've tried to keep myself honest to that too. Whether or not I have succeeded, only God knows.

# CHAPTER 1

## UNEQUIPPED

"Barbara, you are not equipped." The preacher looked straight at me and paused to let it sink in. I felt flooded with relief to hear it said out loud. I was about to be ordained as a Lutheran pastor, and I knew with dreadful certainty that I wasn't up to it. Tom, my pastor and beloved mentor, continued with his stark advisory. Not equipped to preach and teach. Not equipped to care for God's people. Not equipped to bear witness. Not equipped to serve as an example of holy living. I had to restrain myself from nodding like a bobblehead doll.

He turned to face the little group of people who had come from Saints and Sinners in Baltimore. Ordained today, I would be starting my ministry with them in exactly one week. They sat together off to one side, looking uncomfortable in this unfamiliar church, Good Shepherd in Wilmington, Delaware, where Gary and I were members. They looked at their feet as Tom informed them that they had just called a pastor who was not equipped for the job. And they were not equipped, either, to be the congregation they were supposed to be. We would disappoint one another and hurt one another, he warned. Like a marriage, this relationship could not be sustained by good feelings and good intentions alone;

those would be forgotten soon enough. We would have to practice patience and forbearance and forgiveness.

Unequipped.

I stood up to make the promises I was not equipped to keep. The bishop loomed over me, his face red and shiny with sweat over his heavy brocade robe. He read each charge and then looked over his glasses, pausing for my response: "I will, and I ask God to help me." Then his face broke into a broad smile as he waved my clergy colleagues forward to surround me for laying on of hands. They surged out of the front rows, red stoles festive over their crisp white robes. I knelt and they moved in close around me. I felt the heat of their bodies in the tight circle, then the pressure of their hands on my head, my shoulders, my arms and back, until I felt almost crushed with the weight of all their blessing. Finally, as I stood again before him, the bishop spread his arms wide and declared, "Let it be acclaimed that Barbara Melosh is ordained a minister in the church of Christ!"

The very next Sunday I would be standing at the altar of Saints and Sinners, raising the cup and bread to bless Communion for the first time. It had been years in coming—decades, if you counted my years out of church and then my slow, stuttering return. Then five and a half years of seminary, fitted into what was already a full-time life. I'd stayed on as a professor even as I'd become a part-time student too. I'd finished my course work at seminary in December, gotten the last round of approvals for ordination, and finally taken the plunge to retire from the university. Then there had been months of uncertainty, as I waited for a place to practice my new profession.

University colleagues and friends kept asking me how the job search was going. I had to keep explaining there was no job search. Instead, I'd been accepted into the call process. That meant I'd been assigned to one of the fifty-some Lutheran bishops in the United States. To my relief I'd landed in my home synod; it could have been anywhere. Our bishop was in charge of the next step, matching me up with a congregation. Would-be pastors were strictly forbidden to seek out congregations on their own, and congregations too had to wait for candidates proposed by the bishop. And the bishops weren't just employment brokers; the language of "call" affirmed that we were all working under divine direction. Connected to one another as "church," we didn't make these decisions alone, but shared a process of discernment—a word with an ancient pedigree. It meant finding the way forward through prayer, reflection, consultation, and conversation, a process guided by . . . well, we averred it was the Holy Spirit. For pastors and congregations, "call" affirmed that our relationship was more than a contract between employee and employer. We were joined by a covenant, pledging to support one another for the sake of the ministry we shared.

Marian, the assistant to the bishop (or matchmaker), met with me to discuss the congregations I could consider. One of them was Saints and Sinners, a small, struggling congregation about a mile from Baltimore's Inner Harbor. What had once been a busy commercial center around the port had become a deteriorating zone overrun with drug dealers and crime. In the last twenty years the Inner Harbor had become a thriving tourist destination and retail emporium, and the blocks of row houses nearby had become newly attractive to affluent residents. Now real estate agents and developers were eyeing the adjoining neighborhood around Saints and Sinners, and their longtime blue-collar community was becoming a desirable destination for younger, more affluent, more transient people.

I felt an uptick of interest. Many of these newcomers were Gen Xers, young adults who were the subjects of much ecclesial scrutiny and strategizing. Mostly "unchurched" but often self-declared seekers, "spiritual but not religious," they were the mission field of our time, and my people! Granted, I was no longer unchurched and no longer young, but I had a long resume as a seeker. As a professor I was used to being around young adults and knew something of their struggles and aspirations. Maybe I could be a bridge between this congregation and the new neighbors around them.

I did feel a flicker of alarm as Marian described their recent history. The congregation had nearly closed, and more than once. Their profile registered the weariness of long decline. Queried about their activities, they had written, "We have had to sharply focus our cumulative energies towards keeping our doors open," and "Again, we have been through a struggle for mere survival." Invited to list their successes over the last thirty years, they responded, "Keeping the church doors open despite the hard times." When the questionnaire directed, "Identify three congregational mission goals for your congregation for the next five years," they listed one: "To stay open!" Whatever else could be said for them, they knew how to stay on message. Getting them to widen that focus, I guessed, might be a formidable task. Would they be on board for it? I noted uneasily too that two out of their last three pastors had gone down in flames.

I felt filled with misgivings, and I could well imagine they would feel the same about me. They had told Marian they wanted a young man. Their most recent pastor had been fresh out of seminary like me, but without a twenty-year detour from church or a career in godless academe. He'd moved into the parsonage with his young bride, and they'd promptly delighted the congregation with one child and then a second. The Saints had been stunned and bereft when he left after three and a half years.

Gary and I undertook a stealth reconnaissance. The next Saturday morning we cruised down the interstate, about an hour-and-a-half drive from our home in Wilmington. The exit near Saints and Sinners sent us onto a wide street pocked with potholes and lined with small row houses. The streetscape was drab under the overcast October sky, with only a few scraggly trees to break up the brown and gray and dull red of buildings, sidewalk, and pavement. I noticed the bars on almost every corner, along with a couple of pizza places, a barber shop with a red and blue striped pole, and an ice cream parlor with Erline's Beauty Shop on the second floor. A battered sign marked an American Legion post, with a matching VFW hangout across the street.

A block away from the church, Gary backed into an empty space. I had been counting on urban anonymity, but as I slammed the car door shut and zipped up my jacket, I saw we had already been sighted. Behind a screen door an older woman stood observing us, her expression guarded. Her hair was in rollers, and she wore a faded housedress. I smiled and offered a half-wave. She looked back at me, unsmiling, then stepped back and shut the door. I was jarred by this unfriendly reception, but told myself that if most of the neighbors were this vigilant, I'd be safe walking around alone at night.

Saints and Sinners was across the street, a redbrick building with a steep slate roof topped with a cross. A wrought-iron gate enclosed a wide slate porch; a marble planter in front of it was inscribed "The Manse," nineteenth-century parlance for parsonage. It was attached to the church itself, I saw. If I came here, I wouldn't even have to go outside to get to work. That would be a welcome relief after years of arduous commutes. Or would it? Suddenly I was remembering tales recounted by veterans of parsonage living: property committees balking at repairs; members banging at the door at all hours, or even using their keys to walk in uninvited. Just about every story of parsonage life included the one-word summation: fishbowl.

On the corner of the building an aluminum-framed marquee held a signboard declaring "A Warm Welcome Awaits You Here." Next to it was the church door, heavy oak with ornate wrought-iron hinges. Beyond it we saw a metal door propped open. On the sidewalk, a hand-lettered poster on a rickety sandwich board read "Country Bingo." Whatever that was, it didn't seem to be drawing a crowd. Not many people were out on this blustery morning. A jogger in electric-blue spandex trotted past the door, and a young woman in sweatpants walked by without glancing at the sign. I was tempted to peek inside, but we were already on forbidden territory; I couldn't risk an encounter with congregation members who might remember later that I had been snooping around. So we ducked around to the other side of the building, the better to scope out the manse.

It was an imposing building, its red brick trimmed with peach-tinted marble, and by far the grandest house in the neighborhood. Marian had declared it the nicest parsonage in the synod, with seven bedrooms and hardwood floors throughout. I was eager to get a peek. But as we crept around the building, we found mini blinds shuttering every window. Checking out the exterior, we saw that the congregation wasn't quite keeping up with maintenance. Most of the basement windows at street level were cracked, glass held in place with duct tape. On the back side of the parsonage, the window trim and eaves were covered with curls of badly peeling paint. The brick wall that ran along the alley had planters built into the top, filled with tangles of dried weeds. Three battered trash cans were crowded onto the porch. And alas, no parking space. I would be trawling for spaces with the rest of the neighborhood.

Having lurked as long as we dared, we crossed the street to explore the large park that faced the church. We discovered an Olympic-size pool drained for the season and, tucked into one side of the park, a basketball court with broken pavement. The back side of the park held a soccer field bordered with nets next to a baseball diamond. Railroad tracks formed the back boundary of the park, and beyond them, cars and trucks droned by on an elevated stretch of the interstate. This area was secluded, shielded from the main street by the hill that crested in the middle of the park. It might be sketchy at night, I thought with a twinge of disquiet. There was some trash blowing around, and the trees were festooned with ragged plastic bags. But someone was clearly attending to upkeep too; freshly painted metal trash cans had been placed along the paths, and some well-tended shrubs and plants were growing in raised beds. A little sign next to one of them read "Friends of Wayside Park."

My nose twitched with an odd, acrid odor. On the far side of the park, we discovered the source: a playground with a badly charred climbing structure and a partly melted molded plastic slide. Whoever had done this was no friend of Wayside Park, or of the Friends of Wayside Park. We stood there uneasily for a moment, speculating on what the park revealed about the neighborhood. It bore the marks of heavy use and of some neglect, along with determined renovation—and this trashed playground seemed like a disturbing sign that not everyone welcomed the changes.

We headed down a side street to check out the rest of the neighborhood. Built close to the sidewalks, some of the row houses were unpainted brick; many were covered with gray siding molded to resemble stone. Gary recognized it as Formstone, a patented siding popular in the late 1940s and 1950s; Baltimore was known for it. Many of the Formstone-covered houses had displays of artificial flowers in the street-level windows, with aluminum chairs set on the sidewalk; the brick houses had pots outside their front doors, filled with chrysanthemums and pansies.

The sun had come out, and on just about every block someone was out on the sidewalk with a circular saw, working on some home-improvement project. Many houses had building permits displayed in the windows. A few had been gutted, their brick facades punched with cutouts for windows. On others, rooftop decks were under construction, some of them multilevel structures accessed by vertiginous-looking metal steps. The more recently renovated houses all had brick fronts; it seemed that newcomers were shedding the signature Formstone. These changes signaled a neighborhood on the upswing. But I wondered how longtime residents felt about the newcomers who were tearing off the siding that an earlier generation had deemed an improvement. And those rooftop decks—how did they register with neighbors who sat on their front steps to escape the heat?

More than siding was being replaced in the neighborhood. We noticed a large stone church building with arched windows and crossed the street to read the marquee next to the wide wooden door. There was nothing posted on it, though, and then we saw the mail slots; the building now housed apartments or condos. I looked up to the circle of stained-glass above us, facing east. It had probably lighted the altar when the place housed a congregation. Saints and Sinners had nearly closed a few years ago, and suddenly I imagined its brick and marble building divided up for condos, the developers enticing prospective buyers with "Hardwood floors, views of the park, stained-glass windows in many units!" I felt a swell of indignation on behalf of Saints and Sinners, surprising myself; I hadn't even met these people yet, let alone cast my lot with them.

My stomach was rumbling, and my feet hurt. We spotted a corner bar ahead and consulted the menu—pub fare updated for the newcomers, with bacon cheeseburgers vying with spinach salad and butternut soup. We went inside to claim barstools at a small round table overlooking the street. We asked for the local beer, and laughed when we found out it was called "Resurrection." A good omen? As we clinked our bottles together, I wanted to think so.

That Sunday, I enlisted a confederate to advance the reconnaissance deep into the heart of Saints and Sinners. Zoe, my colleague and longtime friend, had followed my turn to ministry with bemusement and unflagging support; she eagerly accepted the assignment to check out the Saints that Sunday at worship. She drove up from her home in Washington, D.C., bringing along her winsome three-year-old daughter. True to their promise on the marquee, the Saints gave them a warm welcome. Undoubtedly it helped that Zoe had showed up with Mia as bait; declining congregations universally yearn for more young families. Still, it was reassuring to know they could reach out to strangers. And it seemed like a good mark for the Saints that their musician was African American, in this mostly white congregation and neighborhood.

Our first meeting with the Saints was supposed to be an informal occasion, with Gary and me both invited to meet the committee charged with vetting candidates. Dave, their leader, had made the arrangements in a few phone calls—dinner at a chain restaurant supposedly halfway between Baltimore and Wilmington. In fact, it was fifteen miles from Saints and Sinners and sixty miles from us. For two excruciating hours, Gary and I strained to make conversation. When I asked Dave about the newcomers in the neighborhood, he snorted, "Yuppies." Chuck, the council president, looked uneasily in my direction and protested, "C'mon, Dave, they're not all yuppies." Dave ignored him. Charlene was probably in her forties, with strawberry-blond hair and a shy smile, but she seemed ill at ease and spoke only when we asked a direct question. Jill, a tall, young-looking eighteen-year-old, got through the whole evening without making eye contact. Betty had a kind, grandmotherly face and a warm smile, and she made valiant efforts to talk with us. But she too seemed uncomfortable. Were they just shy, not used to dealing with strangers? It seemed like more than that. They loved the young pastor who had left, and probably they were still feeling sad about his departure. Or maybe they just didn't like me.

The next week I went to the church for an official interview with the call committee and the council, scheduled for a weeknight when we could meet under cover. I rang at the side door and Dave led me into the parlor, a large, dimly lit room with lamps set around on little tables. A long couch with a scrolled back stood along one side, with matching chairs set around in a circle; they were all covered with pristine white brocade. The room smelled dusty; it was probably closed up except for special occasions. We got down to it; the Saints and I both had agendas. Mostly they wanted to know how I would bring in more people, especially young families. I wasn't quite sure how we would come up with those, since they admitted that people like that were not only scarce in the congregation but also thin on the ground in the neighborhood. Most residents were older people who had been there a long time, or young single people passing through on internships or grad school or other temporary gigs.

I probed for more information about the two pastors who had left in storms of conflict. I had pictured the first one as a left-leaning community organizer; the profile had indicted him for "community activism." But it turned out that he'd upset the congregation with his campaign to preserve the neighborhood firehouse, hardly (on the face of it) a hot-button issue. But maybe they just felt like he hadn't paid enough attention to the congregation. After him they had called a woman pastor, their first. She had disturbed them by sheltering homeless men in the parlor and then deeming members of the congregation unchristian for objecting. I admired her bold response to Jesus' own mandates, though it seemed as if she had gotten out there on her own without the support of the congregation, with predictable consequences. And then there were the dogs. Apparently, she had taken in large numbers of them, and stashed bags of dog food in the basement, which had soon been overrun with rats. They lamented the extensive property damage in her wake. The dogs had trashed the manse grounds and floors, and they'd had to redo the parlor after its use as impromptu shelter and office space.

I felt a jangle of dissonance. On one hand, they didn't seem unreasonable or bent on stirring up trouble; they were measured in their criticisms of these pastors. If anything, they were probably conflict-averse, even passive to a fault. On the other hand, this congregation had gotten mad enough to boot out two of its last three pastors. And it wasn't as if those were different people—all but one of the members of the call committee had been around for years.

The meeting ended with a quick tour of the church building and manse. Eager to check out the parsonage—my future home?—I barely registered the classrooms and fellowship hall in the basement. We headed down the passage that connected the church to the parsonage. Dave fumbled for light switches, revealing generously proportioned rooms with high ceilings, a brick fireplace, a 1950s kitchen with metal cabinets and newer-looking linoleum. Upstairs were four bedrooms, and another floor above that had three more rooms tucked under the eaves. It felt solid and well built, if a little shabby around the edges, with peeling paint and water-stained ceilings in some rooms. Our footsteps echoed through the empty rooms. I felt stirred by the faded grandeur of the place, redolent of the history of Saints and Sinners and its generations of pastors. But it was daunting too. How would Gary and I even furnish this huge house, let alone make a home for ourselves amid these ghosts?

Then Dave led our group back through the hall into the church. He threw open the oak doors to the sanctuary, with its rows of carved oak pews flanked by stained-glass windows. On one side was a pulpit raised up like a crow's nest on a ship. The altar was a few steps up, against the wall, and over it was a half-sized statue of Jesus extending his arms in welcome. Elaborate carving decorated the pulpit, pews, lectern, and wooden panels behind the altar. The darkened wood and dull red pew cushions gave the space a gloomy air in the dim light, but I could imagine it was lovely in daylight, with the stained-glass windows set aglow.

I drove home feeling puzzled and uneasy. They probably felt the same about me. I wasn't feeling the chemistry that usually signaled a good match, whether in work or love. But should that matter? I did feel oddly drawn to them, touched by their resolve and persistence through years of struggle. We weren't an obvious match, the Saints and I, but maybe that meant we were right for each other. They needed somebody who could help them connect with the strangers moving in around them. Someone like me?

Then our courtship hit a snag. The call committee had come to hear me preach at a congregation some distance from Saints and Sinners. It was the first Sunday of Advent, and this meant that as this Sunday's Gospel reading in the lectionary (a list of Bible passages for each Sunday of the church year), by custom the basis for the sermon, I'd drawn John the Baptist ranting in the wilderness. I flailed around and finally found inspiration from a sermon by the eighteenth-century Puritan preacher Jonathan Edwards. I explained who he was and laid out his compelling take on the text. As it turned out, the Saints did not find this edifying. (What was I thinking?) In fact they were taking a step back. They were not dumping me outright, but they didn't want to go ahead until they heard me preach again.

I was cut to the heart to learn I'd flunked the sermon test — and furious too. I knew I had a lot to learn about preaching — more than I knew then — but I came to it with skills honed over twenty-five years of teaching and writing. The sermons I had preached elsewhere had been warmly received, even showered with accolades. And in seminary I had gotten an A in homiletics! But none of that mattered. The fact was that my sermon did not connect with them — or worse, actively put them off. I considered walking away. Maybe the Saints and I were just not a match. Or was I letting pride get in my way? I decided to go ahead. This time I'd preach at my home church in Wilmington. We set the date for the second Sunday after Christmas.

I had long deemed December the cruelest month. It always found me working overtime to close out the semester, even as the calendar lurched toward Christmas, with its to-do lists for shopping, baking, office festivities, home decorating. It had gotten even worse these last few years, now that I was both a student and a professor. At seminary I was writing papers and studying for finals. At the university, I got the other side of it: student pleas for clemency; stressed-out colleagues; and looming deadlines for reports, end-of-year budget reconciliation, and more; followed by grading papers and exams, and then calculating final grades. This time around, the usual overload was freighted by my constant awareness that I was doing all these things for the last time.

At the seminary in Philadelphia, I handed in my last paper and then walked around the campus in a ritual of leave-taking. I climbed the wrought-iron stairs to the library mezzanine to sit in my favorite spot in the stacks. Next I went into the chapel and plunged my hand into the cool water of the deep stone baptismal font. Then I crossed the street to the Wawa, the convenience store that was an unofficial annex to the seminary, to buy a valedictory coffee.

At the university I met my last classes and sent the students off with bittersweet good-byes. I had felt weary of academic life for a while, and so I felt some relief, even a giddy sense of release. Still, I was daunted to come to the end of it, reflecting on all the years I had given to this first calling, and feeling no little unease with the uncertainties of the next one. The last month had been a series of last things: my last seminar, my last undergraduate class, my last faculty committee meeting. I graded final papers and exams and posted grades for the last time.

I cleaned out my office, packing up books and files and setting out bag after bag of paper for recycling. It felt liberating to get rid of it, but sobering too. All those conference papers and proposals, minutes and correspondence, syllabi and lecture notes, class lists and grade sheets—documents of the days and semesters and years of my life here. As I discarded most of it, I felt downhearted. In the end, what did it amount to? I had forgotten most of these students, served on committees whose work came to nothing, thrown myself into heated debates over questions that now seemed trivial. I felt grief and anger at the wrangles and bureaucratic obstacles of academic life, and more than that, dismayed at the evidence of my own misguided priorities and squandered energy. Then again, I had relished the energy of intellectual exchange and had often found satisfaction and joy in teaching. I'd loved much of my academic life, and been well rewarded for it. Someday, I thought, I'd regard it with more equanimity than I felt now, and with gratitude for the rich and meaningful work of this first vocation. But as Zoe helped me pack the last few boxes and waved as I drove away, I felt stunned and apprehensive.

On December 26, 2004, a week before I was scheduled to preach, an obliterating tsunami hit South Asia and Africa. Tens of thousands of people, many of them children, were sucked to the ocean floor. The news was filled with appalling photographs and stories, as people searched desperately for the missing, and rescue operations tried to reach the millions without shelter, food, or water. The Scripture for January 2: Jeremiah's proclamation of God's promise to turn mourning into joy, and the enigmatic prologue from John: "In the beginning was the Word. . . . the light shines in the darkness, and the darkness did not overcome it." It was an apt initiation into the impossibility of preaching. Absolutely nothing I could say would be adequate. But I had to say something. It was my job as preacher to find God even in this devastation, or at least to lead a search party into the darkness, shining a weak flashlight in front of us. With my hands gripping the pulpit to still my trembling, I stood up that Sunday and poured out my heart, all the grief and agonized questions and deep undefeated hope. Then I sat down, wrung out but calm. If I hadn't connected with the Saints this time, we were done—and so be it.

The call committee gave thumbs up, and we headed into the last lap: interview weekend, when candidate and congregation meet face-to-face. On the appointed Saturday night, the Saints assembled to fete us with a potluck in the fellowship hall, with tables covered with casseroles and salads, cakes and pies and cookies. As we ate and talked, I kept trying to imagine myself as their pastor. If this worked out, I would be teaching confirmation to those three eleven-year-olds; visiting Lois, who'd gestured to the scarf around her head as she explained she had cancer; burying John, who held us rapt as he told about landing on the beaches of Normandy on D-Day. I felt warmed by the shy smiles that greeted us around the room—though also out of place and acutely aware that Gary and I would be outsiders among the blue-collar Saints.

I felt relieved to spot one person who seemed more like me and my tribe. Georgia wore a boiled wool blazer with a contemporary design. Her hair was stylishly cut and colored; she looked to be about my age or a few years older. She told me she had grown up in another part of Baltimore, raised her kids in the suburbs, and then exchanged the big house and lawn for a row house right down the block. I sensed she would be an ally and a crucial link to the new neighbors. And it seemed that the Saints had accepted her; she even moved freely in and out of the kitchen, probably the inner sanctum here, as in other congregations.

Taut with nerves, I didn't sleep well in the hotel that night. My stomach was roiling as the service began on Sunday. When it was time to preach, I climbed up into the pulpit with a sense of doom. Up there the air seemed thinner, though it was only three steep steps from the floor. I took a deep breath and looked over the congregation, then launched into the sermon. Their faces were unreadable, but at least I didn't see anyone scowling or crossing their arms over their chest. One older man was asleep, snoring lightly, but maybe he always dropped off during the sermon. Afterwards, Dave led Gary and me into the parlor to wait out the vote. I eased off my shoes and slouched into one of the brocade chairs. Gary offered me a section of the Sunday paper, but I was too wired to read. Downstairs the congregation was making the decision that would either certify my new vocation or send me on a U-turn back into the call process.

I wasn't sure how long these votes usually took, but just as I was beginning to feel as if this one had gone on for too long, Chuck, the council president, appeared at the door and grinned as he announced, "White smoke." Downstairs in the fellowship hall, the congregation broke into applause. I looked around the room. A couple of people looked away—no votes, probably. The kids looked excited. Georgia wore a triumphant smile; she caught my eye and nodded encouragingly. Around the room, I saw faces lit with smiles and what looked like hope.

Called! After these years of preparation and months of waiting, I was going to be a pastor. *Their* pastor.

Three weeks later, I stood up to make the promises of ordination. I felt exhilarated, thrilled to be at the edge of this new life. Buoyed by all the people who'd come to support me. Filled by the music and language of the ordination service. And oddly braced by the preacher's refrain, as he kept repeating what I deeply knew.

I was not equipped.

# CHAPTER 2

## ARRIVAL

Unequipped. The word kept ringing in my ears. But ready or not, I was launching my new life as a pastor exactly one week after my ordination — and not just any week. My first Sunday was Palm Sunday, the start of Holy Week. That was the home stretch before Easter, a week both feared and revered among pastors. It had seemed a little reckless to start then — the busiest week of the year — and I'd hesitated at first. But I was eager to get under way and to join the Saints for Easter, the biggest celebration of the year. In most congregations the attendance was double or triple that of an ordinary Sunday, so I'd likely get to meet everyone even remotely connected to Saints and Sinners.

Lutherans follow the same playbook as Catholics and Epis-copalians, meaning we're heavy on the ritual, and Holy Week is filled with rites that happen only once a year. Plus, it's a week with three or four or even five services instead of one, and each one includes a sermon. Saints and Sinners did a medium-intensity Holy Week: an evening service on Holy Thursday, two services on Good Friday, no Easter Vigil (a beautiful but complicated three-hour extravaganza held on Saturday night), and two services on

Sunday morning—one at sunrise and another at eleven o'clock. Each of these services had its own script and staging, and a whole cast of characters to be mobilized to make it work, from the altar guild to whoever did the bulletins. But what unnerved me the most was the preaching: five sermons to prepare for that first week.

We had decided not to sell our house in Wilmington right away. At least for a while, we'd operate with two households, with me in the parsonage and Gary trying out what would work for him. He had quit his job to help me get started in Baltimore and then to concentrate on writing; he had a book in progress. I was relieved we weren't trying to move all our stuff from Wilmington and get the house ready to sell. But that meant we had to find enough furniture and kitchenware to set up housekeeping in the manse. At least we didn't have to measure anything. Whatever we found would be swallowed up in those large empty rooms.

Gary was masterminding the move. He'd ordered a mattress and box spring for the oak bed frame we'd found at one of the secondhand places and arranged shipping for the book cases, rocking chair, and tables, but none of it would be delivered until after Easter. And we had yet to tackle the kitchen. We could cull some things from our house in Wilmington, but would need dishes, silverware, pots and pans. With Holy Week bearing down, I had no time to worry about any of that; I would have to improvise with whatever we could bring to Baltimore in one trip. We wedged a small foam-rubber futon into the Subaru, and I added a few changes of clothes, a towel, sheets, and pillow, along with a bag of dog food, a coffee pot, and a mug. Our black Lab Shadow lumbered into the back seat, and we left for Baltimore.

When we pulled up in front of the manse, I opened the car door to let Shadow bound out. George and Constance appeared on the sidewalk as if summoned by some unknown signal. Constance was the congregation's financial secretary and reigning matriarch. I had met her when the council had interviewed me, and had seen how others deferred to her. George was about her age, probably early seventies, lean and fit, and a man of few words; I'd yet to hear any from him, though they'd both attended my ordination service. I was surprised and relieved to see them; we hadn't known for sure what time we would arrive, so I hadn't expected a welcoming committee. While I fumbled with the keys to unlock the gate and the front door, George and Gary slid the futon out and then angled it upstairs. Constance disappeared and then returned with a bowl of water for Shadow. I set it down on the kitchen floor. The black and white linoleum tile looked freshly waxed, and the counters gave off a faint smell of cleanser. On the counter was a gift basket with a bottle of wine, a bag of coffee, dish towels, and a couple of mugs with "Saints and Sinners" printed on them. George and Constance stood at the door for a moment looking awkward as I thanked them, then backed out, telling me they'd be over at the church if we needed anything.

I set up the small coffee pot on the kitchen counter and opened one of the 1950s-era metal cabinets to stash filters and ground coffee, and set the mug I'd brought next to the two from the gift basket. I hung up two new dish towels, tan and yellow stripes. The early afternoon light flooded through the clean windows, and the kitchen and adjoining laundry room smelled of new paint. Standing at the sink, I looked over the backyard, a rectangle enclosed with a brick wall. They had gotten rid of the battered garbage cans that had filled the back porch. I saw that they were now off in the far corner, partly shielded by a wooden fence. Against the wall of the Sunday school building, the thick canes of some venerable rose bushes were starting to put out tiny leaves.

I joined Gary as he walked around to assess the space and plan where the furniture would go. A few things were already in place, discards from members or previous pastors probably. Under the crystal chandelier in the dining room was a long oval table covered with a lace rectangle; looking closer, I saw it was a panel curtain. Underneath, the lovely old wood was scratched and stained with large white blotches, like lichen spreading over rock. There weren't any chairs with it, so we went downstairs to the church basement to poke around. I brought up a few wooden chairs with red vinyl seat covers, 1950s vintage. Gary spotted a bonus find, an armchair covered in orange faux leather with only a small tear on one side. Once we had wrestled that up the basement stairs, he dug the car keys out of his pocket and headed out for the ride back to Wilmington. He would manage the rest of the move while I launched into Holy Week.

I headed out the door to scope out the closest corner store and found it a couple of blocks away. I browsed the aisles to pick up milk and cereal amid the vast array of junk food. The traffic was brisk, with people coming in and out for snacks, cigarettes, and lottery tickets. Across the street, a coffee place catered to the young and hip; when I stuck my head inside, a line of twenty-somethings were calling out orders for smoothies and designer coffee over the racket of blenders and an espresso machine. There were bars on every block, some with menus posted in the windows. On one corner, a battered metal door was propped open to reveal a few solitary drinkers on stools. Neon signs from beer companies blinked behind the bar. I was guessing the bartender didn't mix cosmopolitans. Four doors down the street, I saw "Paul's Place" stenciled in gold across a curtained window, with hanging ferns giving it a kind of retro-yuppie vibe. The nearest apple-tinis, though, were probably not to be found for a mile, where Gary and I had seen a former foundry that housed a trendy restaurant and wine bar.

Back at the manse, I stashed my rations and then made the first walk of what would be thousands of repetitions: barely a minute, all indoors, that took me from the manse to my church study. Through an interior door to a short set of steps, through another door to the church, down the side aisle of the sanctuary, through the sacristy (where Communion ware was stashed), and down a short hall—and I'd arrived. I took a long look around; I'd be clocking hundreds of hours here, planning worship, poring over sermons, counseling parishioners. The long, narrow room was painted in a flat white, dingy and peeling in places, with one corner streaked with water stains. The single large window framed a spare urban vista, overlooking the alley and the brick and cement of row houses that backed up to it. Shelves covered one wall, with plenty of room for the ministry books I had been accumulating, even without clearing out the five or six shelves that were already filled with a puzzling assortment of stuff. Bags of fair-trade coffee and tea were lined up on three of the shelves; looking more closely, I saw they were all well past their expiration dates. Several large plastic grocery bags were stuffed with crosses fashioned of needlepoint; there were hundreds of them, all identical but for the yarn—lavender, white, yellow, pale blue, pink, red. Frosted white Christmas balls stenciled with an outline of the church took up another shelf, and yet another was filled with mugs like the two in my gift basket, printed with the congregation's tagline: "Saints and Sinners: A warm welcome awaits you here."

The sun was low over the row houses—time to forage for dinner. I went downstairs to the church's kitchen to borrow a bowl and spoon for tomorrow's breakfast cereal, and another bowl for Shadow's food; I had forgotten her dishes. I clipped on her leash for a walk around the park, then tied her outside Mike's Pizza while I ordered a calzone. I was glad for her company as I opened the cardboard box in the kitchen and hunched over the calzone, oozing with mozzarella and tomato sauce. As darkness fell, the kitchen looked bleak under the harsh light of the fluorescent fixture. I pulled the orange chair under the living room chandelier and tried to read in the dim light. At ten I took Shadow out again, keeping to the edges of the park closest to the street; I wasn't sure if it was safe at night. As I crossed the street back to the manse, I felt a little start to see my name on the marquee: "Rev. Barbara Melosh, Pastor."

Inside, my footsteps echoed on the oak stairs, with Shadow's toenails clicking in counterpoint. Gary and I had set up the futon in the back bedroom. At home, folded up as a love seat, the futon had taken up most of one wall in Gary's study. Here, flipped out for a bed, it looked like a small dock listing on the edge of a large pond. I spread a sheet over it and tried to prop up the pillow for a backrest. Shadow gave me a quizzical look and then settled down on the carpet with a sigh. I read for a few more minutes before turning off the overhead light. I lay in the dark listening to the rumble and wail of the freight trains that crossed the neighborhood and wondered how long it would take before this felt like home.

Constance and George were already in place when I got over to my office the next morning, coffee mug in hand. They occupied the long, narrow room across from my study, nearly filled by a massive wooden table and matching chairs—the council room, according to a plastic label screwed to the door. The walls were lined with black-and-white photographs of past council presidents, with curling labels indicating their names and dates of service. They were a serious-looking bunch, all men, dressed in suits and ties and regarding the camera soberly. When I examined them more closely later, I noticed the gallery didn't include Chuck, who was Constance and George's son and the current president. In fact, it seemed as if time had stopped in this gallery somewhere in the mid-sixties.

Constance sat at one end of the heavy table, its surface covered with papers and files, along with an old-fashioned ledger and an adding machine threaded with a roll of paper. Most of the chairs were heaped with stuff, with more items stacked on the floor along the walls: several toolboxes, flyers and worship bulletins, bags of yarn, piles of knitted afghans, a large manual typewriter perched on a rickety metal stand. She had been sorting through bills, it seemed, and entering figures in the ledger. Across from her, George dozed in one of the wooden armchairs, a newspaper folded across his chest.

I was wary of Constance, even a little intimidated. I knew that she played a major role in the congregation's life, and that finding a way to work with her would be essential. Constance looked a bit like the schoolteacher she had been, tall and slender, with a self-contained air and a serious expression. Her large brown eyes were watchful behind her glasses, her barely lined face framed with soft gray curls. I felt sure that nothing escaped her attentive gaze and, perhaps, her stern judgment.

She waited a tactful few minutes and then offered to go over the congregation's photo directory with me. She pulled up a chair next to mine and set the directory on the desk, its paper cover curled with use. It was ten years old, so Constance had updated it with penciled notes in her deliberate handwriting. Many of the photos were lightly crossed out, with dates of death or "moved" written underneath. I peered at the faded photos as she moved her finger along the rows. She paused at the photo of an elderly couple in their Sunday best; he was wearing a badly knotted tie, and she was in a flowered dress: "These were Bernice's parents; she lives down the street now, taking care of her older sister." Farther down the page, she pointed at another photo and explained, "Margaret was a Strobel, married into the Fitzgeralds, and her daughter married a Lutz. Their kids were baptized here, but we don't see them too often." "Let's see, Elmer was council president for several years. He died a year after this picture was taken, but Edna's still living in their house down the street."

She went slowly, looking up every page or so to make sure I was following. A headache started to tighten across my forehead. How would I ever keep track of all these relationships? But one thing was all too clear: in this dense matrix of shared history, I was an outsider, even an alien. Members of congregations often talked about their "church family," but the Saints really were family, most of them, kin by blood and marriage. Almost every member was related to at least one other member who wasn't in their household. And without exception, they all had ties to the neighborhood. Quite a few members lived in the row houses that lined these streets; most of them were longtime residents, with a handful of people who had moved in recently, like Georgia. Others had grown up here but had moved out of the city to inner-ring suburbs; Constance and George were among them, though I found out later that they still owned Constance's parents' house a few blocks from the church. One way or another, everyone had roots in the neighborhood—everyone but me and Gary.

Still, I was living here now, and I set out trying to make a place for myself in the neighborhood. It was really two neighborhoods, as Gary and I had seen on our first reconnaissance: the older one beloved of the Saints, and the new one emerging as gentrification made inroads. As the new resident of the parsonage, I had a claim, however tenuous, to citizenship in both of them. At least that was the upbeat version. I didn't want to dwell on the other possibility, that I'd find myself straddling the fault line between them, without a place in either one.

I was already learning that Saints and Sinners registered very differently with old and new neighbors. One afternoon I stopped to talk with a guy sitting on his front steps with a beer cracked open next to him. He was probably about my age, fifty-something, wearing work boots and a Ravens jacket. When I introduced myself as the new pastor at Saints and Sinners, he gave me a faintly amused look. "Yeah, I know. Moved in a couple days ago, right? Your husband's tall, white hair? So where's he gotten to?" He lived across the street from the older woman who'd spied Gary and me on our stealth reconnaissance. I was impressed, and a little unsettled. These people made it their business to know what was happening in their neighborhood.

Then there were the Gen Xers, often in evidence in the park, trotting behind jogging strollers or walking their dogs. One evening I struck up a conversation with a young woman, blond hair gathered into a ponytail, as Shadow greeted her shambling golden retriever. When I introduced myself as the new pastor at Saints and Sinners, she looked puzzled. "You know," I continued, "the brick church on the corner." She shook her head apologetically, ponytail bobbing.

"Over there," I pointed.

She looked across the park and said uncertainly, "Oh, yeah. I guess I did know that was a church. So it's still open?"

I was taken aback. I knew the Gen Xers would be a tough crowd, but I hadn't realized we'd have to work to get them even to notice we were here.

Palm Sunday! This time last week, I was getting ready for my ordination service, and now I was about to lead the Saints in worship for the first time. This service starts with a procession of all the able-bodied. The assembled worshipers are supposed to listen to the story of Jesus' triumphant entry into Jerusalem, get their palms blessed, and then stride into the sanctuary waving palms to the strains of a vigorous hymn in march tempo, traditionally "All Glory, Laud, and Honor." I finished blessing the palms, and then there was an awkward pause. It occurred to me that people were waiting for some cue that I didn't know how to give. Marie was overhead at the organ in the choir loft, so I couldn't signal her to start the music for the processional hymn. Finally she did start playing, but still no one moved. I was so nervous that I plunged down the aisle ahead of the cross.

Whatever I was supposed to do, that wasn't it—the cross always goes first—but the Saints straggled behind me anyway. We were supposed to be marching in a triumphal procession, but between my being out of place, the listless pace of the marchers, and the feeble singing, it wasn't coming off. What was wrong with these people, anyway? As I turned at the front to watch the last of the marchers taking their seats, I realized that hardly anyone was singing, because their hymnals were in the racks attached to the pews. Anyway, with a palm frond in one hand and bulletin in the other, who could hold a hymnal? As I had prepared this service, I'd pored over my notes from seminary and "Leaders' Guide to Worship," the manual for pastors that supplemented the hymnal, but as I'd planned the service I hadn't thought to give it a test walk-through.

Already I had a feeling this was going to be a humbling experience.

When it was time for the sermon, I gathered my robe in one hand and gripped the oak railing with the other as I climbed the steps to the pulpit. I paused a beat as I got to the top, looking over the congregation. About 25 people, most of them elderly, were scattered around the room. This sanctuary could probably hold 150 people easily, and their usual total attendance for two services was around 70. But I'd been warned in the hiring process that the Saints would not welcome any changes to their Sunday schedule. This early service was billed as "traditional." That could mean a lot of things, but here it meant that worshipers wanted organ music and familiar hymns.

I didn't recognize most of the people on the pulpit side, but then Betty caught my eye and smiled warmly. She'd been at that first awkward dinner, and I remembered her husband, Harry, from the potluck. The large man next to them was probably her brother—Constance had mentioned him. On the other side, Georgia sat by herself a few pews from the front, with Constance and George installed behind her, about halfway back. Dave sat by himself in the last pew. A few minutes into my sermon, George nodded off, joined a few minutes later by a rumpled guy on the other side. The others listened stoically. I was a little unnerved. Lutherans are notoriously restrained, but this crowd could have taken any of them down at the poker table; not a single gesture or facial expression betrayed any response to the sermon—unless you counted the two who had dozed off.

Only ordained ministers are allowed to preside at Communion, so I was doing that for the first time today. I had rehearsed several times that week in the empty church, marking the steps I would take to get to the altar, then practicing the gestures and memorizing the words. I kept stumbling on the steps, undermining what little confidence I could summon. Couldn't I even walk up stairs without falling on my face? After several mishaps, I'd knelt down to examine the steps more closely. The problem was their nonstandard proportions. The risers were unexpectedly short, and the treads too narrow even for my size-7 foot. To add to the challenge, the treads extended an inch or more over the risers, and that's what had been tripping me up. I had been catching the toe of my shoe on the overhang and then pitching to my knees. Once I'd managed to negotiate my way to the altar, more hazards awaited. The narrow altar was fixed to the wall, and so in order to face the congregation during the consecration, I would have to pivot back and forth to pick up the bread and wine. Simple enough, except the steps were graduated in size, like a rectangular wedding cake. At the top, a step or two to the side would send me reeling off the edge.

Lutheran worship involves lots of participation from laypeople, with an assisting minister designated to offer prayer, help with Communion, and keep an eye out for any glitches along the way. Luckily for me, Bruce, the assisting minister assigned for that day, was well schooled in the job and used to working in the space; he knew his way around the altar and took me firmly in hand to forestall any mishaps. He was tall and heavily built, with a ponytail streaked with a few strands of gray. When it was time for Communion, we went up to the altar together. I picked my way up the steps, head down to monitor my feet. Bruce's feet were huge, barely contained in battered running shoes, but he moved to the altar with athletic grace and the ease of familiarity. He picked up the missal, a heavy, well-bound book with the service in large print, and held it in front of me. Just as I was about to begin, he whispered, "Pastor, don't step backwards." When I turned to lift the large wafer in blessing, and then the chalice, he warned again, "Stay right there." I was touched by his vigilance and unnerved too. I was guessing he'd seen at least one pastor go sprawling. To keep myself in place, I imagined that my feet were nailed to the floor.

The Saints lined up to pick up little plastic cups on a side table, then threaded through the side door and up the steps to kneel at the altar rail. I worked my way down the row, placing wafers in their open hands. Behind me, Bruce carried a chalice in each hand, pouring wine or grape juice into the little cups. I turned at the end of the row to retrace my steps for the next group. But the first communicants, though, were still on their knees, looking up at me expectantly. I looked back at them blankly. I stood there for what seemed like long minutes. Just as I was feeling a nervous giggle bubbling up, Bruce came up next to me and said in a low voice, "They're waiting for you to dismiss them."

Ah, yes! I even remembered what this was called: "communing by tables," meaning that they waited for everyone at the rail to be served and then stayed until excused. This was an old pattern, one we'd used at my own childhood church; we would receive the bread and wine, then kneel in place until the pastor dismissed us with "Go, and sin no more." As a kid I remembered hearing it with a sinking heart, certain that I'd be sinning again all too soon—maybe even before we got home for Sunday dinner (my two younger brothers could be very annoying in the backseat). I cast about for some alternative and settled on "Go in peace," trying for an authoritative tone. I realized a beat too late that this was the dismissal used at the end of the service, but to my relief it got the Saints moving. They hauled themselves to their feet and shuffled out as the next row made their way down the rail. Repeat, and this time I knew how to get them off their knees.

After the service, I stood at the back of the church to greet people. "Pastor," most of them called me, and each time I felt a momentary confusion, catching myself before looking around to see whom they were talking to. A few of the women exclaimed over my alb, the white robe that Lutherans wear when leading worship; mine had lace insets in the sleeves and bottom hem. Others smiled and asked how we were settling in at the parsonage. No one said anything about my sermon or my awkward missteps.

Mostly, I realized, they were relieved. They were still reeling from the body blow of losing their beloved pastor, a young man whom they'd embraced as an honorary son or grandson. Some, I had heard from Marian, had hoped he'd come back, right up until the vote to call me, even though he was now the pastor at another church. For more than a year, they had been without a full-time pastor. Most congregations falter a little in these periods between pastors, sometimes losing members and confidence; small congregations are especially vulnerable, and Saints and Sinners had come close to closing more than once in their recent history.

They couldn't really afford a full-time pastor, but they were determined to have one anyway. And now they had gotten one. They didn't care about my degrees or my theological insights, my years of experience as a professor, my story of midlife conversion or my passion for language. At most, they were prepared to put up with it all, if that was what it took to get a pastor in place. What they wanted was to come to church—this church—on Sunday, to take their familiar places in the pews, to worship the way they'd done for years, with the people they'd known for years. They'd endured months of uncertainty and unwelcome dealings with ecclesial authorities. So today they seemed weary but relieved, glad to get a handshake at the door from someone they could call pastor—*their* pastor.

At eleven o'clock the procession was ragged again, but at least I didn't get out ahead of the cross. I had thought to instruct people to get hymnals so we could sing as we went; a few did, but even so, it wasn't easy to juggle the books and the palms. We did get a little boost of energy from a handful of kids who were happy to wave their palms and delay their confinement in the pews. It helped to have a bigger crowd too—maybe sixty or so, more than twice as many as the congregation at the early service. Chuck was there, with his wife and three boys; and Charlene (who'd been on the call committee) with her husband. Jill, who'd been the youth representative on the call committee, was there with her family. Fifteen strong, the Feldmans commanded the first two pews right under the pulpit, startling me a bit; it was almost unheard of for Lutherans to submit to sitting in the front, let alone to stake out that territory by choice. Gary and Zoe were sitting a few pews back from the Feldmans; I felt glad to have my own little posse amid all these people I didn't know yet. After the service, I felt elated and then suddenly wiped out—the Sunday crash I'd learned to expect from the year I'd spent with a congregation as a seminary student. But now I was the pastor, on day one of Holy Week. Just one week before, I had taken the vows of ordination, and now the bishop's solemn question echoed in my mind: "Before almighty God, to whom you must give account . . . I ask: Will you assume this office, believing that the Church's call is God's call to the ministry of Word and Sacrament?"

I had answered, "I will, and I ask God to help me." I could already see I was going to need all the help I could get.

# CHAPTER 3

## HOLY WEEK SPRINT

Holy Week. On Monday I woke up with a start, disoriented to find myself on the futon in the parsonage. I had been so consumed by planning for Easter that I'd hardly had time to feel the strangeness of being a pastor now, after a long path through seminary and, before that, years of wavering as I wandered back to church.

In some of those years out of church, Easter had barely registered with me. For one thing, the date moved around capriciously; one year it turned up in March, another in April. I knew it was coming up by the displays in the grocery story: jelly beans and chocolate eggs, and Easter egg dye next to cases filled with egg cartons. I held on to a few remnants of it, observing Easter as a church-free celebration of spring—a festive late breakfast with muffins or coffee cake, and colorful dyed eggs nested in Easter grass. Other years, Easter had felt like a line in the sand. I'd been abashed to show up at some church for the first time on that Sunday, along with other short-timers and slackers; yet not attending on Easter seemed like too final a declaration that I was done with church.

As I careened through the week, it felt saturated with memory, a palimpsest of other years of Holy Weeks and Easters showing beneath the wash of this first Holy Week at Saints and Sinners. Growing up in church. Leaving church. Coming back to church. And now I was in charge of a church, and sprinting toward Easter.

On Thursday was the first service of the trifecta—er, the Triduum, it was called, Latin for the Three Days, the sequence that builds to Easter Sunday. Holy Thursday commemorates Jesus' last supper with the disciples, and traditionally it includes foot washing. Jesus himself commands the disciples to do it in the reading for the night, but nonetheless, many congregations don't comply. It's archaic, some argue, a practice that no longer fits our context. We don't get our sandaled feet dusty on unpaved roads like the people of first-century Palestine, so offering a foot washing is not part of our rituals of hospitality. Besides, people are squeamish about their feet. We're ashamed of our own bunions and warts, our calloused skin and gnarly toenails, and repelled by the thought of other people's nasty feet. Touching someone else's feet is done only by professionals—at a pedicure or a podiatry exam—or in intimate encounters.

But that awkwardness is telling—maybe just what we need. Foot washing disturbs our boundaries in ways that open us up to Jesus' radical demands. Jesus uses foot washing to show his disciples how to serve one another with unflinching intimacy, to offer one another the humble service usually done by servants, and to be willing to receive that service from equals or superiors. In seminary, we'd been encouraged to get our congregations to brave it. But this was a hard sell at most congregations, and I couldn't see myself springing it on the buttoned-up Saints when I'd been their pastor for less than a week. I hadn't considered that they might already do foot washing, but there it was, I was surprised to see, listed in the bulletin for Holy Thursday. I had seen the big pottery basin and pitcher in the sacristy, and I went downstairs to the kitchen to hunt down some towels.

Back in my study, I looked over the program again and noticed that there weren't any worship assistants listed. Lutheran services typically include readers for the lessons, assisting ministers for prayers and Communion, acolytes to light candles, altar guild to set up, greeters to welcome worshipers, and ushers to direct the congregation at Communion. Attendance would probably be light tonight, so we could double up on some of these jobs; but I'd need some backup. Special services confront a congregation with an unfamiliar order of worship, and this one involved moving people around for the foot washing. Then I checked the Friday bulletins: same thing, no one listed for either the noon or the evening services. My anxiety ratcheted up a notch. Mildred was the person who assigned the worship assistants, I remembered, so I called her to find out who was on for Thursday and Friday. She answered cheerily, "Oh, yes, I schedule everybody for Sundays." So, what about special services? "Pastor does that!" I swallowed my irritation. How was I supposed to know that? But this was no time to instruct the Saints on clear communication and shared ministry. Instead I started punching in phone numbers until I'd cobbled together a bare-bones roster.

Holy Thursday usually turned out only the faithful few, so I figured tonight would reveal the hardcore saints. The Feldmans filled their two pews at the foot of the pulpit. Halfway down the other side, Constance and George had staked out their seats. A few others were scattered in the pews, about twenty-five altogether (fifteen of them Feldmans by blood or marriage). At the foot washing, six or seven people came up. Eleven-year-old Bobby was one of them, to my surprise. He was Marge's son, one of the Feldman clan. Most people found this at least a little awkward, and I had hardly expected an adolescent boy to volunteer for it without a trace of self-consciousness. But as I took his foot in my hand and poured water over it, Bobby acted as if this were perfectly natural. It seemed that church was part of his family identity, what it meant to be a Feldman. I wondered a bit wistfully what that was like. My mother had brought me and my brothers to church and done duty as a Sunday school teacher and more, but Dad ordinarily kept his distance, and a certain unspoken tension had surrounded the whole matter of churchgoing.

Good Friday. In preparation, the worship space had been stripped bare in a solemn ceremony that took place at the end of the Holy Thursday service. By a little after noon, the congregation barely broke into double digits. Huddled in the mostly empty sanctuary, our small gathering shared a quiet service of lament and somber meditation. For that evening I had decided to tweak the planned service with an overlay of Tenebrae, the Service of Shadows.

I'd first experienced Tenebrae in 1989, at Mighty Fortress, the Lutheran church I'd been attending in Washington, DC. This time I was thinking about making it official, actually joining a congregation again. I had never been to an evening Good Friday service before, but it seemed like what an actual Christian might do to prepare for Easter. So I had decided to try it out.

It was growing dark as I walked through our Capitol Hill neighborhood to get to Mighty Fortress. I sat by myself in the dimly lit sanctuary, one of a small assembly of worshipers scattered through the cavernous space. The rich purple cloths of Lent were gone, and the big cross mounted on the front wall was covered in black. Seven large candles glowed in the darkness, set in a row on the bare altar.

The centerpiece of the service was a dramatic reading of the passion of Christ from the Gospel of John. After each episode, one of the big candles was extinguished. In the darkening church, I felt drawn into the story as never before, gripped by the emotional intensity of John's long account: Jesus is betrayed, then arrested in the garden, then denied by Peter. In the courtyard, Pilate wrestles with his uneasy conscience, appealing to the crowd to release Jesus as a Passover act of mercy; instead, they demand that he release Barabbas, a thief.

Again Pilate tells the crowd he sees no reason to condemn Jesus. What then should he do with him? I gave a start when a woman two pews in front of me leapt to her feet and shouted, "Crucify him!" Around me others yelled, "Crucify him! Crucify him!" For the first time, sitting in that dark church, I understood that we were that crowd, the ones who crucify Jesus, over and over again.

I was wrung out by the end, relieved when a reader solemnly intoned Jesus' last words: "It is finished." I felt for my purse next to me, getting ready to leave. Then suddenly the lights went out, plunging the church into darkness. A long silence followed, long enough that I started to feel uneasy, uncertain about what we were supposed to do. Then suddenly I was jolted by a shock wave of sound like cracks of thunder, the noise building to an ear-shattering crescendo. Silence again, followed by a loud bang like a heavy door slamming. Then silence again, and in the darkness, the small congregation began to whisper the Lord's Prayer.

A single spotlight came on, following a male figure as he labored up the center aisle with a wooden cross laid over his shoulder. He set it on the steps leading to the altar, and again we waited in silence. After a few minutes, people began to stir. Someone flicked the lights back on, and we made our way out the heavy wooden doors. No one spoke, and the pastor was not at the door to greet us as he usually did. I walked home pensively under the yellow street lights, held in the spell of Tenebrae.

This first Good Friday at Saints and Sinners, I knew I couldn't pull off a full-bore Tenebrae at such short notice. But when I'd discovered an old brass candelabra in the choir loft, I couldn't resist trying to graft Tenebrae onto the Saints' Good Friday service. I searched the sacristy and found seven candles. I managed to assemble most of the needed readers, appealing to Zoe and Gary to fill a couple of key roles. We'd had no time to rehearse, and it was too late to recruit ringers to yell "Crucify him!" from the pews. I had enlisted Bobby and Marie to execute the special effects. He would douse one candle at a time, and then slip down the side aisle to dim the lights gradually. Marie would work the lights up front, making sure to click off the spotlight on the choir when the last candle was extinguished.

Bobby pulled on his alb and took the candle snuffer off its hook to place it near his seat. He listened closely as I described what I wanted him to do with the sanctuary lighting and the sound effects. I'd brought up some large baking sheets from the kitchen to rattle for thunder; I explained that this was supposed to recall the earthquake that occurred as Jesus died, according to one of the Gospels. Then there was the Great Noise—I'd learned that was the name for the sudden startling boom in the darkness, representing the door of the tomb slamming shut. I set a heavy book on a table in the back, for Bobby to slam down after he'd switched off the last light in the sanctuary.

This twist on Good Friday would be a novelty for the Saints, and I hoped it might deliver the same emotional wallop I'd experienced. Instead, the effect was muted by a series of miscues and bad timing; in the end, the Saints were probably more baffled than awestruck. Bobby got the candles snuffed and overhead lights dimmed according to script, but it wasn't yet fully dark outside, and some light leaked in through the stained-glass windows. When the time came to kill all the lights inside, I had to dash across the front to douse one stray spotlight, only to realize that someone had left a light on in the hall. The sound effects fizzled like fireworks in a downpour. Bobby shook the cookie sheet energetically but it produced only a faint rattle. The Great Noise followed all too promptly, a muffled thud that was barely audible from the front. Bobby's father hauled the cross up to the front for a finish that restored a little of the intended gravitas. As the congregation dispersed, I thanked the participants, told myself that it hadn't been a complete disaster, and resolved to make it better next year.

Easter. I stumbled over to the dark church, groggy and grouchy. Was anyone really going to turn up at six thirty in the morning? And what was the point of having a sunrise service indoors? I had puzzled over the service that the interim pastor had planned, an odd riff on the Easter vigil. That service was supposed to start with a bonfire (or some facsimile thereof; a lot of congregations settled for a flame on a big candle) and a procession into a dark space that represented the empty tomb. Here we would gather in the narthex and move into the darkened sanctuary with candles. George arrived and turned on the lights. I turned them off, explaining that the service was supposed to start in darkness. He looked baffled and shrugged. When I stepped away, he turned the lights on again. I turned them off. He waited a beat and turned them on.

Soon there were more than twenty people crowded into the narthex—the eight-thirty regulars, it seemed. Just as I was about to begin, I looked up and saw Zoe coming up the stairs. I gave her a quick grin; I hadn't imagined she'd drive an hour before dawn to get here for sunrise. I turned off the lights again, telling the little crowd that we were starting in darkness to represent the empty tomb. I reached up to light my small candle from the tall thick candle I'd moved from the front of the church. When everyone had a light, we straggled into the pews.

We were supposed to hear the readings in the dark, but when George turned on the lights again, I let it go. The altar was laid with a beautiful white silk cover bordered with gold, and surrounded by Easter lilies. Their heavy scent filled the air. As the sky lightened, the stained-glass windows glowed with color. When I stood to read the Easter Gospel, I felt wrapped in the wonder of it: Mary Magdalene at the tomb, where she mistakes Jesus for the gardener, until he speaks her name. As I held up my arm in blessing at the end, I felt blessed myself—my first Easter with the Saints!

At the back, I looked expectantly to the small congregation, waiting to greet people as they left. But half of them were moving to the front of the church, clustering around the lilies. Puzzled, I watched as they looked appraisingly at the plants, then made their selections and began to carry them off. They'd paid for them, I knew; the bulletin had a couple of extra pages acknowledging their donations, lilies purchased in honor of the living and in memory of the departed. I'd figured, though, that the lilies would stay in place for a few weeks, or at least until the eleven o'clock service was over. But I saw that's not how it worked here, as the Saints bore their trophies triumphantly down the aisle and out the door.

A few minutes before the late service, Martha was bustling around the altar, moving lilies to fill the gaps left by the absconders from the early service. Tall, big, blond, and loud, Martha stood out among the otherwise reticent Saints. She was head of the altar guild *and* the kitchen crew, a woman to be reckoned with. I had warmed immediately to her thousand-watt smile. She was serving as assisting minister that day, and as she came back to the sacristy to put on her alb, she warned, "Pastor, stay away from the lilies." I gave her a quizzical look. Did she think I was going to snatch one or two from the display before the service? No, she was thinking of my new alb; even brushing against the orange pollen on the stamens, she advised, would set a stain that was impossible to get out. (She was right about that, I discovered when I ran afoul of a lily another year.)

By eleven o'clock the church was nearly full. As Bobby lit the candles and Marie launched into the prelude, I looked over the congregation with rising excitement. No doubt some of these people were members who didn't attend regularly, or relatives of regulars who'd pressured or pleaded with them to come on Easter. But at least some of them, I felt sure, had to be newcomers checking us out. I remembered my own long citizenship among the "unchurched." Now I was on the other side, and here was my chance to reach out to people who might be finding their way back to church.

Or was it? I remembered how I myself had been undone by Easter and sent careening out of church, again. I'd been on the verge of joining Mighty Fortress, and had especially looked forward to our Easter visit to my parents. Our son, Mike, was three years old and had been thrilled when we arrived on Saturday and got ready to dye eggs. He'd watched as I measured white vinegar into small cups and then showed him how to tear open the little strips of cellophane and drop the tablets of dye into the vinegar. His eyes widened as I poured in water and the colors bloomed. I'd taken the photo that captured him with my parents; Mike was looking up at my father with sheer delight as Dad beamed at him, his face creased in a huge smile, almost a rictus, stretching his gray skin tight against his bones. By then he was mortally ill, sixteen years on dialysis, and being overtaken by an accumulation of complications: bone loss, heart disease, and more. On Mike's other side, Mom was smiling broadly, her face lit with joy. In front of them, the eggs were scattered on a drying rack arrayed in Easter pastels: aqua, green, yellow, peach, pink, and lavender.

On the way to church on Easter morning, I decided I should give Mike a quick briefing about what was coming. I'd been bringing him to the early service at Mighty Fortress most weeks, shamelessly bribing him with the promise of donuts afterward. But this service would be different. First Lutheran, my childhood church, would be filled with people today, and the service would be more celebratory—and longer—than the subdued early worship we usually attended at Mighty Fortress. I felt chagrined to realize how little I'd done to tell Mike about church or faith or God. I'd been silenced by my own questions, unsure of what I believed myself, let alone how to explain any of it. So I turned around to face Mike in the backseat and announced, "Today's a special day in church! It's like a big party because we're happy that Jesus came alive again after he was dead!" Gary didn't quite suppress a derisive snort, and I was cringing myself at my own fake-sounding mother-speak. Then too Mike had to find all this baffling. Sure enough, he looked confused and asked, "How did he get dead?"

I groaned inwardly. The obvious question, and yet I was totally unprepared for it. "Ah, well," I stalled, "remember the parade at church last Sunday?" Mike had come with me for Palm Sunday at Mighty Fortress, and we'd joined the ragtag procession at the church door, waving our palms as we followed the cross down the center aisle. "Remember how everybody was so happy to see Jesus, so they all cheered and brought palms to give him?" Mike had loved that part. When we sat down, he had lashed the pew in front of us until I had to pry the palm out of his fist. "But then," I went on, dropping my voice with dramatic portent, "those people got so mad at him in just one week that they killed him." I regretted the words as soon as they were out of my mouth; this story was too stark for a three-year-old. Mike looked stricken. His lip trembled, and tears welled up in his eyes. "Did he get shot?" he asked fearfully.

This was a recent preoccupation, since the Martin Luther King Day celebration at Mike's preschool. On Presidents' Day Mike learned that Lincoln had also gotten shot. Somewhere he'd heard about Kennedy's assassination. He had concluded, not unreasonably, that public figures were routinely felled by bullets. Gary and I were attempting, so far unsuccessfully, to moderate this perception, since Mike had developed an outsize fear of assassins that might be lurking in our Capitol Hill neighborhood.

I hesitated. Until now, I'd never fully considered what a gruesome story this was. Still, sooner or later—maybe even at church today—Mike was going to hear about the crucifixion. I took a breath and prepared to continue. Gary cut me off with a hard look and said, "OK, that's enough. We're here."

Inside, the choice seats (in the back) were already filling up, so we hustled down the side aisle to find an open pew. The organ swelled with "Jesus Christ Is Risen Today," and I felt a lump in my throat as Dad belted it out, along with a little reflexive embarrassment. As a kid and then a self-conscious teenager, I had been mortified by his Easter zeal. At six feet three inches, Dad was conspicuous anyway, and when he commenced his off-key bellowing, I felt certain that everyone was staring at us. He claimed to love the hymn, but his high-volume rendering also seemed addressed to my mother, payback for making him come to church. As always, she let out an annoyed sigh and looked ahead stonily.

I had come to worship today filled with longing, wanting to feel stirred anew in this place I'd once loved and then left behind. Instead I felt out of place and disheartened. I wanted Mike to know what it was like to belong to a congregation, but how could I give him that experience when I was so conflicted myself? I watched him with my mother, awash in my own memories of Sundays in these pews. He was squirming next to me as the sermon started, then giggled and quieted down. I looked over to see Mom surreptitiously passing him something—foil-wrapped chocolate eggs. Suddenly a whiff from her purse reached me, that familiar smell of leather mixed with face powder and mint. She would open her purse every Sunday when our pastor stepped up to the pulpit, finding a little treat to keep us still through the sermon—a peppermint, a Life Saver, sometimes even a half-stick of gum. Mike shot me a glance, thrilled to be scoring candy in church. I smiled and pretended I didn't see what they were up to.

I felt stifled in the hot room, the air heavy with perfume and the cloying sweetness of the Easter lilies clustered at the front and on the window sills. A headache started to pulse in my temples. We stood for the Apostles' Creed, and I choked on the words. It felt like a loyalty oath I couldn't affirm, flooding me with memories of my adolescent angst. I had struggled to find some way to assent to these unlikely propositions, then felt bereft and guilty when I failed to parse the arcane language into anything that felt remotely plausible. And now here it was again, rearing up like a stone wall shutting me out.

I had spent years inching my way back to church and then leaving again. But now I'd heard the Easter story anew, telling it to Mike, and it felt like another unscalable barrier, this keystone of the whole wildly improbable Christian story. I had tried to believe it, tried to find a place for myself at Mighty Fortress, but why? Abruptly I stood up and stumbled past Gary and down the side aisle, out the side door into the hall, down the stairs to a bathroom.

I locked myself into the far stall and leaned against the wall. It was all exactly the same, the pink tiles in an offset pattern, the air freshener with its acrid orangey smell, like baby aspirin. I felt a rush of memories of the minor scourges of Sundays: dress shoes pinching my toes, garters pressing into my thighs, too-tight skirt cutting into my waist. I collapsed into sobs for a few minutes, feeling ridiculous. It's only church, I admonished myself. And I wasn't in high school anymore. I didn't have to do this. I straightened up and pulled off a length of toilet paper, ordering myself to stop crying.

Overhead I could hear the opening bars of the Communion hymn, "Just as I Am, without One Plea." I had to get back upstairs. If I timed it right, I could slip back into the crowd as people moved around for Communion. I looked at my swollen face in the mirror, cupped my hands and tried to repair the damage with cold water, then blotted my face with brown paper towels. I got upstairs just as our row was returning from the altar and slipped between Gary and Mike in the pew. Gary reached over and squeezed my hand, and Mike cuddled next to me.

Back at the house, no one said anything about my abrupt departure from the service. I was grateful for my parents' discretion, or maybe it was just our stalwart family code of repression. Either way, I was relieved not to have to try to explain what I didn't understand myself. We sat down to scalloped potatoes and ham, the dishes we always had for Easter dinner. The afternoon stretched into restless boredom and the sickish feeling of too many jelly beans.

The next day we packed up the car. Mom and Dad stood on the porch and waved as we backed down the driveway. As usual, I felt a pang as I turned to watch until they were out of sight, wondering, as always, if this was the last time I would see Dad.

It was. He died six weeks later.

"Jesus Christ Is Risen Today" was the opening hymn at Saints and Sinners that first Easter, and I steeled myself for it. Always, it evoked memories of Dad. As Marie played the opening measures, I thought of him and felt the unlikeliness of my own life all over again. Me, a pastor? I wondered what my father would have made of it, my going back to church and then to seminary. Next to me, Martha belted out the hymn, wildly off-key; I had to concentrate to stay on pitch myself as she veered from one register to the next. The small choir stood at the piano, their voices leading the congregation.

I'd labored over my sermon, wanting to unsettle the regulars to hear the story freshly and to engage people who weren't usually in church on Sundays. I began by evoking the scene of Mary Magdalene coming to anoint Jesus' body, only to find the tomb unsealed and empty; the body, she must have thought, had been stolen and desecrated. The empty tomb, for that first witness, was a sign of terror and violation. In our own lives, that empty tomb echoes still with all our own grief and losses, our fear and loneliness, the violence of our own world. But finally, the empty tomb is a sign of resurrection: not a violated grave, but an open door, the testimony that Christ is alive, and the promise that death will not have the last word. As I preached, the rustling in the pews faded until my words were the only sound in the room. When I finished, the silence continued for a long moment. Had my words touched something in my hearers, or set them pondering? Maybe they were just thinking, "What was *that* about?"

As people filed out at the end, I tried to size up the crowd and sort out regulars, occasional attendees, and newcomers. I spotted a likely prospect who didn't seem to know any of our regulars; she looked to be about forty and wore a green linen jacket, gold jewelry, and an air of upper-middle-class assurance. She shook my hand firmly and told me she was visiting her daughter, who had moved here a couple of months ago. "Right down the street," she said pointedly, clamping a hand on her daughter's arm. "Carolyn hasn't been to church since she left home for college, but maybe that will change now that you're right on her doorstep." Great, just the endorsement I needed to woo a skeptical young adult. I smiled and met Carolyn's eyes with a rueful look. Mothers! So bossy! Carolyn gave an opaque smile in return.

As the last few people dispersed, I looked up and saw the Feldmans lining up across the front of the church. Agatha, the matriarch, was front and center, flanked by her two daughters and their husbands; the "boys" (her two adult sons) were behind her, with the kids arranged by height in the front row. (Agatha's daughters Marge and Sally were no longer named Feldman, having taken their husbands' last names, but I'd already realized that the Feldman identity trumped any mere marital contract. Besides, it was clear that around here, husbands were more or less incidental; the matriarchs were in charge.) Watching them smile for the camera, I felt moved to witness the importance of "church" in their family rituals. At the same time, I felt a little disquieted by their sense of entitlement. Their command of the front pews, and now their claiming the church as a backdrop for the family photograph, felt a little proprietary, even clannish. So far I'd experienced them as cordial, if not quite friendly. I felt curious and a bit wary. If only by their sheer numbers, the Feldmans were a force to be reckoned with.

I was giddy with relief and exhilaration as I went back to the parsonage with Gary. I'd made it, my first week! I felt buoyed by the full church. If even ten of these newcomers or infrequent attenders came back next week, we would be kick-starting the renewal desperately needed here. I couldn't wait for next Sunday, and the opportunity to ride the surge of Easter.

The Sunday after Easter always includes the story of doubting Thomas—perfect for a pastorally sensitive appeal to skeptics and seekers! He was the disciple missing in action on that first Easter evening, when the risen Christ appeared to the disciples. When Thomas heard about it, he declared he wouldn't believe it until he'd seen it with his own eyes and touched Jesus' wounded hands and side. The next week, Jesus shows up again and admonishes Thomas, "Have you believed because you have seen me? Blessed are those who have not seen and yet have come to believe."

For as long as I could remember, I had recognized myself in Thomas and struggled with the demands of blind faith. So my sermon anointed him as the patron saint of seekers. Doubt was not shameful, but an honorable part of the life of faith. God had given us the gift of reason; all our questions were already known to God, and already accepted by God.

On Sunday I got ready for worship with rising anticipation, eager to extend this welcome to the skeptic. I knew Easter Sunday had the highest attendance of the year and I didn't expect the church to be full; I did hope, though, that we would have some return visitors. So I was surprised, and then crestfallen, when worshipers were scattered thinly in the pews—all of them regulars, not a seeker among them. When I preached about the virtues of doubt, I saw blank looks and a few furrowed brows. The Saints were probably wondering what to make of me, a pastor who not only defended doubting Thomas, but admitted that she was a doubter herself.

I slunk back to the parsonage and poured a cup of coffee. Then I remembered that I'd heard pastors refer to this first Sunday after Easter as Low Sunday; it seemed lots of people took a week off after Easter. None of our occasional visitors or newcomers had turned up for a second look, either. So maybe Easter wasn't the outreach opportunity that I had imagined. But we were surrounded by new neighbors, most of them young adults. They were everywhere—in the park, the grocery store, the pizza places, and the bars. Everywhere but here, that is; but that could change. Surely some of them would respond to our appeals. Time to ramp up our efforts and bring them home, saints and sinners all.

# CHAPTER 4

## VIGIL

After Easter I set out to meet our homebound members, the congregation beyond the church walls. Irma was next on my list, and I felt a pleasant sense of purpose as I put on a black clergy shirt and attached a collar. Then I went to the sacristy to restock my Communion kit, a black leather-covered box containing a small bottle for wine, a plastic cylinder for a stack of Communion cups, and a round metal container for wafers. Finally, I stopped by my study to take *Occasional Services* from the shelf, a compact book bound in dark green leatherette with gilt-edged pages and a gold cross stenciled on the front. Equipped!

*Occasional Services* had been a gift from a Lutheran mutual benefits association (now defunct), bestowed on me and other students in seminary. It was part of our ritual of initiation, taking place during our two-week Greek intensive, a crash course meeting six hours a day (plus homework!), five days a week. It was the custom for a few sympathetic alumni and alumnae to appear midway through the intensive, offering support and commiseration.

They handed out goodie bags filled with bottles of juice, cookies, and energy bars; then they began to open up the cardboard boxes they'd hauled in, ceremoniously offering each of us our own copy of *Occasional Services*.

As I had thumbed through what turned out to be a kind of secret manual for pastors, I had felt anointed and unsettled at the same time. Between its green covers were protocols for funerals, graveside services, installations and ordinations of pastors, and a long list of other events that might be commemorated (occasionally, of course) in worship, from Laying of a Cornerstone to Thanksgiving at the Disposition of a Church Building. It seemed that no detail of church practice went unregulated. Guidelines for Ringing Church Bells, for example, explained "certain customs" to be observed, including the occasions that called for a single bell, a peal (three to five bells), or a plenum (all five bells, until the largest had been rung seven times). Who knew? This compendium of protocols was daunting, yet it was reassuring to know that I could turn to *Occasional Services* for answers.

I'd made heavy use of *Occasional Services* through my stint of clinical pastoral education (CPE). Required of all Lutheran ministry students in training, CPE was a full-bore initiation into the challenges of working with people in crisis. I'd done mine as a chaplain intern at the Hospital of the University of Pennsylvania (HUP), a high-profile teaching and research hospital; patients came from all over the region to receive highly specialized treatments or to participate in clinical trials. My beat had been neurology, including the neurosurgical intensive-care unit, the seizure unit, and a large neurology unit where dozens of patients were treated for everything from spider bites to brain tumors. During the day, we also took turns carrying the beeper that hospital staff used to summon a chaplain when needed. Most often, that meant a call to the trauma unit, a separate section of the emergency room where the most severely injured patients were treated. In addition, our group of six interns also provided twenty-four-hour coverage for pastoral care; every six days, one of us would take night duty for the whole hospital. I hadn't yet had the occasion to ring church bells, but *Occasional Services* had proved invaluable at the bedside, in the trauma bay, and in the waiting rooms where anxious family members gathered. So, as I set out to visit Irma at the Golden Years Care Center, I went equipped with *Occasional Services*, confident it would provide whatever I needed.

An unseasonable heat wave had slammed the city. Though it was only the first week of April, the temperature soared to the mid-eighties. The air conditioning in my car wheezed against the humidity, a feeble current of lukewarm air wafting out the vents. I saw the sign for Golden Years Care Center and turned into a cracked driveway alongside what looked like a converted motel. I opened the car door to a rush of hot muggy air and ran a finger under my plastic collar to peel it off my neck. Under my silk blazer my clergy shirt was stuck to my back like plastic wrap, and I could feel a trickle of sweat running down my side.

Dave had offered to meet me at the nursing home to make introductions. He hadn't said much about it, or about anything—he was notably taciturn even among the Saints, who rarely surrendered more than a few words without strenuous effort on my part. But I had learned that he regularly checked in with members who were homebound or in the hospital. I was often intimidated by Dave's gruff manner, but already had come to depend on him when I needed advice or found myself baffled by the Saints. He had known Irma for years, having grown up in the row house next to hers, a half block down from the church. Irma's sister Dolores still lived there and had been caring for Irma at home until a year ago.

I looked around for Dave and noticed a scruffy-looking guy standing near the door in a worn gray sweatshirt with sleeves torn off to expose beefy arms, his belly hanging over cut-off shorts. Beat-up sandals completed the ensemble. As I got closer, I did a double take. It was Dave, his grizzled hair pulled back into his usual ponytail. Dave had a master's in chemistry and supervised a team of technicians at a local industrial lab. What was with the aging hippie impersonation?

A couple of weeks before I'd managed to get Dave to submit to a conversation that included some exchange of personal information. I had discovered that he was my exact contemporary; we had both graduated from high school in 1968. But he had stolidly avoided the baby-boomer mainstream, the water I had swum in. While I left home to try on late-sixties youth culture in a small liberal arts college, Dave attended the local branch of the state university. In a way, though, he had wandered far from home himself, further than I had, as the first person in his family to go to college. He was one of only a handful of college graduates in the congregation. When the people at Saints and Sinners talked about when they'd finished school, they meant graduating from high school. In 1972 I went on to graduate school to earn a doctorate in what was grandly termed American civilization, a wildly impractical pursuit in a dire academic job market. In the years when I had moved into a collective house, embraced the women's movement, and labored over a dissertation on women's history, Dave had taken the job he still held, married his high school girlfriend, fathered a son and daughter, and somehow managed to get a master's degree along the way.

So what was he doing showing up at the nursing home in an outfit that recalled scenes from my college days? But then again, it occurred to me that Dave might look like a throwback to me, but he would fit right in with the guys who gathered in the neighborhood bars to cheer on the Ravens and the Orioles. Most of the men I'd gone to college with had left behind the counterculture long ago, exchanging their ponytails and denim for expensive haircuts and designer suits; it was blue-collar men, these days, who grew their hair long and embraced grunge. Dave had moved on from the neighborhood in more ways than one, but he hadn't cut himself off from his blue-collar roots. I didn't yet grasp it, but that loyalty and tenacity were both the signature strengths of the Saints and the very qualities that held the congregation in a death grip. Or so I came to believe.

He pulled open the door and led me down the hall past the nurses' station, where a couple of aides looked up indifferently as we turned into Irma's room, shades drawn against the late afternoon sun. She was lying in bed, her eyes closed. I felt a tick of alarm as I saw her chest heaving, her breaths noisy and ragged as she struggled to drag air into her lungs. I had heard it before but hadn't expected it today: Cheyne-Stokes respiration, the labored and intermittent breathing of a dying person. Dave put a thick hand on her shoulder and leaned close to her ear, gently calling her name. No response that I could see. She seemed deep in that end-of-life drift, sinking away from this world.

I wheeled around and went back down the hall to the nurses' station where a woman in flowered scrubs sat at the desk. She was expressionless as I demanded, "What's going on here? How long has Irma been like this?"

"We can't give that information to someone who's not in the family."

"I'm her pastor. Have you talked to her sister?"

"We've been trying to get her in here. We called a couple of times. I told her Irma was on comfort care."

"Comfort care." Somehow I doubted that Dolores would recognize this professional euphemism, translated "the patient is dying, and we're doing what we can to keep it from hurting." I walked down the hall to call Dolores on my cell phone. She was confused and then alarmed when I told her to come as soon as she could. "But, Pastor, they told me Irma was on comfort care, I didn't think she was sick." When I offered to pick her up, she said she'd get a ride from Eileen, a neighbor and a member of Saints and Sinners.

I went back to the desk to talk to the aide again: Brenda, Nursing Technician, according to the name badge pinned over her pocket. She was probably about forty and looked uncomfortable, perspiring a little in the warm hall. She didn't look happy to see me again. I soldiered ahead anyway, letting her know Dolores was on the way. Who's the attending physician, I asked, and will someone be coming to talk to Dolores about what's going on with Irma? Brenda informed me flatly it wasn't the doctor's day to make rounds. I pressed her; couldn't she call him in?

She gave a shrug and pushed herself to her feet, wincing a little in discomfort. As I watched her, I belatedly realized I'd just witnessed a masterful exercise of self-control. She'd been polite, if barely, fending off this pastor who seemed to think she was in a well-run hospital, instead of a cut-rate nursing home. It was time to start passing out supper trays, and there were only three aides working on this long corridor, with ten or twelve rooms on each side and maybe thirty-five patients who needed food, meds, bed-pans, diaper changes, blankets, and more.

Tonight she had me to deal with on top of the usual, as I tried to pry a little more attention for Irma out of this staff, already stretched thin by the look of it. The care here seemed strictly no-frills; that was the way these operations eked a profit out of patients whose care was probably underwritten by Medicare and Medicaid. Likely there was one doc who covered the whole place, to sign paperwork, write prescriptions for meds, and nominally supervise patient care plans. He wouldn't be summoned for some-thing as ordinary as a death watch.

Back in the room, Dave was sitting next to Irma's bed, holding her hand and murmuring softly to her. I went over to Irma's other side and laid my hand on her shoulder, telling her that I was the new pastor at Saints and Sinners and that Dolores was coming soon. Again, no response that I could see. I dragged a chair over to the bed. A cart clattered down the hall. Irma sucked in air with rattling breaths, punctuated by abrupt silences as her chest went still. I found myself holding my own breath until Irma gasped and strained for the next wheezing breath.

Footsteps down the hall, and Dolores tottered into the room. Her stained aqua track suit clung to her round body, and a few hairpins were trailing from the thick silver hair rumpled around her face. She stopped at the foot of the bed, looking at Irma in a daze of confusion. She peered at me as if she was trying to remem-ber who I was, then thanked me for calling. Dave heaved to his feet, and she stumbled into his open arms. Then he let her go gen-tly and set her into his chair.

"What happened to her?" Dolores asked plaintively. But if any-one here knew what was wrong with Irma, they weren't saying. Whatever it was, she was dying now.

Eileen appeared at the door, a stout, capable woman with short dark-brown hair streaked with gray. She had grown up in the neighborhood, a couple of blocks away from the church, then punched the middle-class ticket by becoming an accountant; she and her husband had moved out to the suburbs. Now they were back; most of the newcomers in the neighborhood were Gen

Xers, but a few were empty nesters like them, unloading suburban houses and lawns for smaller row houses in the city.

We settled around Irma's bed for the vigil, a tacit death watch. I sat next to Dolores, asked about her life, listened to the stories as the sun got lower. I got confused more than once, as she talked about growing up in the neighborhood, next to Dave's family. As Dolores reminisced with Dave about their high school years, I realized she was remembering his father, who was also named Dave; this Dave was my age, and couldn't possibly have gone to high school with her. But he just nodded and smiled as she talked, ready to stand in for his long-dead father, if that was what would get her through this night. Dave's silences often unsettled me; that day, they opened the space for Dolores to remember and grieve.

The light faded in the room as the sun set. We fell silent, listening to the hard labor of Irma's breaths, punctuated by long pauses, then another struggle for the next breath. Then a loud stuttering breath, and Dolores exclaimed, "Dave! Is that a death rattle?" He reached over and patted her hand.

I turned to Dolores and took her other hand, then asked if she wanted to have some prayers for Irma. We got up to stand around the bed as I opened *Occasional Services* to the Commendation of the Dying. At the end I gestured for them to place their hands on Irma; I put mine on her forehead and read the words also spoken at funerals. "Into your hands, O God, we commend your servant Irma, a sheep of your own flock, a lamb of your own choosing, a sinner of your own redeeming." Then we turned to one another and hugged. Dolores was crying silently, tears running down her withered cheeks. Dave gently guided her back to her chair.

It was now completely dark outside. An aide came in and dimmed the light over Irma's bed. Eileen got up and left. Dave and I sat down again to keep the vigil with Dolores. We talked a little, then fell into long silences, listening to Irma's breaths. In the shadowy room, my mind drifted and I struggled to stay awake. It felt familiar, this rhythm of the vigil, and I found myself remembering Ray, the first person I'd accompanied to the far edge of life.

Ray had lain nearly motionless in the neurosurgical intensive care unit for days, his chest rising and falling as the ventilator wheezed and clicked beside him. I had gone into his room every day on my rounds, gently rubbed his arm, called his name, and gotten no response; he had never opened his eyes. I was puzzled when Jean, his wife, kept leaving me messages, all of them the same, imploring me to pray with Ray. But how? I felt at a loss, and not only with Ray. Most of the patients on this unit were unconscious. How could I be their chaplain?

One day I arrived when Jean was there with their daughter Sandra. "Chaplain! I'm so glad to meet you! We can't get here every day, and we need to know that someone is praying with him when we can't." Confused, I started to point out the obvious — Ray was unconscious. Just in time, I realized that made no difference to them. If anything, it mattered more that someone would pray with him, to say the words that he couldn't speak. After that, I had stopped by every day to take Ray's hand, whisper a prayer, and sometimes to sing a few verses of a hymn. At first it felt strange to talk and pray with patients who gave no sign of hearing me. Soon, though, it became so familiar that I was startled on the rare occasions when someone answered me.

Ray had esophageal cancer, documented in a chart stuffed with lab reports and physicians' notes; he'd been hospitalized multiple times in efforts to slow down the cancer and treat a cascade of complications. But finally he'd run out of options. Ray had wanted to die at home, and Jean clung to the hope that he could recover enough from the latest setback to be discharged. But as the days went by, even that seemed out of reach.

During our orientation my CPE supervisor had quipped, "No one dies at HUP without an appointment." That wasn't quite true, but the hospital did execute a rigorously controlled protocol for directing patients who were making their final descent. "Do Not Resuscitate" (DNR) orders are widely used in hospitals; at this one, DNR was further elaborated into three distinct categories. DNR-A meant treating a patient to avoid cardiac arrest (but not intervening if the patient's heart did stop). DNR-B meant maintaining current treatments but not adding anything new; Ray was currently in that category. DNR-C was the decision to remove life support, and that was the recommendation Ray's team was now making.

Jean and Sandra asked me to come to the meeting where they would consider this decision. We crowded into a small conference room with Anne, the nurse practitioner at HUP who specialized in "end-of-life care," also known as dying. She started with a detailed review of Ray's medical history. The recitation was unsparing; Anne seemed at pains to emphasize that Ray's condition was dire and irreversible. He was going to die; the question was how.

Ray's wife and daughter understood that; they nodded sadly through the exhaustive summary. Anne was clearly advocating for DNR-C, withdrawing life support. Jean and Sandra forlornly hoped for a natural death—whatever might count as natural at this point, anyway. Taking Ray off life support felt to them like arrogance, interfering with God's action and will. That surprised me a little; Sandra was a nurse, and if removing the ventilator was playing God, so was keeping someone alive that way. Ray himself hadn't been in a position to consent to the ventilator, but his own advance directive had made it clear he didn't want extraordinary measures. Still, actually making that decision on behalf of someone else is a weighty charge, and Jean was struggling mightily with it.

She turned to me, her face creased with worry, and asked, "What does God think of this?" I hadn't seen that coming and stammered that I couldn't speak for God. Jean looked at me plaintively, and Sandra reached over to take her mother's hand. Anne gave me a hard look and said sharply, "Chaplain?"

I took a deep breath and started again. Protestant, Catholic, and Jewish religious leaders all have approved removal of life support in extremis. God's will is for abundant life. What did that mean for Ray? No one thought his present condition allowed Ray any meaningful quality of life, and Jean and Sandra had accepted that Ray would not be able to die at home. Now they were distressed to think that he might die alone; they lived some distance from the hospital, and if they opted to wait for him to die without withdrawing life support, they might not be with him when the time came. If they did decide to remove the ventilator, Anne explained, Ray would die within a few hours; the family could gather and stay with him.

After almost two hours, Jean and Sandra were still undecided, and clearly exhausted. I described the Commendation for the Dying; maybe it would help to have those prayers. Then even if Ray died when they were not present, they could have at least shared this ritual of leave-taking. They brightened a little at this suggestion, and we ended the conference and went to Ray's room.

Around us the intensive care unit was quiet that night; the lights were dimmed and the only sounds were the incessant wheeze of ventilators, the blip of heart monitors, the occasional beeping to signal an empty IV bag or displaced needle, the cushioned steps of nurses moving from room to room. My voice wavered as I started to read the Commendation for the Dying. Then the words steadied me, words of promise and comfort, prayers calling for God's shalom, for wholeness and healing.

Near the end, the rubric instructs, "The minister lays his/her hand on the head of the dying." I reached over the ventilator tubing and placed my hand on Ray's forehead, warm and slightly sweaty under my palm. "Child of God, go forth in the name of God the Father almighty who created you, in the name of Jesus Christ, Son of the Living God, who redeemed you; in the name of the Holy Spirit who was poured out upon you. May you rest in peace and dwell forever in the paradise of God." Jean and Sandra wept quietly. The brief service closes with the same prayer that is said in evening prayer in the traditional liturgy of the hours: "Lord, support us all the day long of this troubled life, until the shadows lengthen and the evening comes and the busy world is hushed, the fever of life is over, and our work is done. Then, Lord, in your mercy, grant us a safe lodging, and a holy rest, and peace at the last."

Jean and Sandra seemed drained but relieved. We hugged, and they left the hospital for the night; they would get some rest and decide what to do tomorrow. My beeper, miraculously silent this whole time, now came to life; over and over it sounded the code for the trauma bay. In between alerts, I hurried to the on-call room to fling myself on the narrow bed for a few hours of sleep.

The next morning, the duty nurse on the ICU paged me. Jean had decided to end life support, and the ventilator would be withdrawn that afternoon. When I got to the ICU after lunch, Jean and Sandra were white-faced and drawn but resolute. Ray and Jean's son and his wife arrived, disheveled and with red-rimmed eyes. Sandra's husband stood next to her, handsome, composed, and deeply reserved. Anne arrived to talk with them again. Alicia kept a watchful eye on them all; petite and blond, she was one of the ICU nurses who had cared for Ray these last weeks.

As we stood around Ray's bed, I opened *Occasional Services* again; I'd bookmarked the prayer used when life support is withdrawn. "God of compassion and love, you have breathed into us the breath of life and have given us the exercise of our minds and wills. In our frailty we surrender all life to you from whom it came, trusting in your gracious promises." The respiratory therapist turned off the ventilator and in a single swift movement pulled the tubing from Ray's throat. Anne had warned that this might produce a loud gasp; when Ray remained silent, she and I exchanged quick glances of relief. The therapist placed the tubing on Ray's chest and covered it with a towel. Heavily sedated, Ray was motionless except for the slight rise and fall of his chest. He might breathe on his own for minutes or hours. We backed out of the room to leave the family to keep the vigil.

I looked at the wall clock behind the desk at the nurses' station. It was four o'clock, but was it early morning or late afternoon? I had been on duty for thirty-six hours, and in the windowless ICU it was easy to blur night and day. I claimed a chair behind the desk and tried to look alert so as not to disgrace the pastoral care service. These noble intentions notwithstanding, I found myself nodding off and then fell asleep, my head on the desk. I jerked awake when Alicia patted my arm to rouse me and pointed to the Styrofoam cup of coffee she'd set beside me. I sipped the acrid brew, trying to clear my head. I was beginning to worry about driving home in such a fog, and yet I wanted to see this through. Around me the nurses consulted quietly, and Alicia went into Ray's room every few minutes.

Sandra came out into the hall and summoned me to the bedside; Ray had just died. She and Jean stroked his still body and murmured over and over, "No more tubes." The family around the bed joined hands as I prayed out loud — *Occasional Services* again, with prayers for consoling the bereaved. Then the little crowd in the room began to disperse. I hugged Jean and Sandra, then staggered out to the parking garage. I felt exhausted and yet oddly exhilarated. *Chaplain.* I knew with sudden clarity that I wanted more of this; I felt hungry to claim the name of "minister," and to meet those in need with the deep resources of church.

So now I was a pastor — Irma's pastor, though she didn't know it — and keeping the vigil at Golden Years with Dave and Dolores. No end-of-life specialists here, or respiratory therapists, or ICU nurses. I didn't know if DNR was written on Irma's chart or not, or if she even had a chart. There wasn't one in the room, and no crash cart in the hall, and no resuscitation team to respond to a code. But these vigils had one thing in common: they took place in the body's own time. For Ray and for Irma, and for each one of us, death would arrive on its own schedule.

As the minutes ticked by, I began to feel anxious about getting back to the parsonage. I felt mostly safe in the neighborhood, thanks to the vigilance of longtime residents who watched the streets; at the same time, I was uneasy about the drug trade still operating on the edges. By 9:00 p.m., parking spaces were scarce, and I was nervous about having to park on the fringe of the neighborhood, where I would have to walk down a couple of blocks filled with abandoned houses and seedy bars. Not only that, I was feeling frayed after five hours in this stuffy room, hungry and tired and longing to get home. It seemed as if every breath might be Irma's last; and yet I knew this could go on for hours, even days. Still, it didn't seem right to leave Dave and Dolores to keep the vigil by themselves. I decided to stay another hour. The three of us sat in silence while Irma breathed in and out, a jagged rhythm.

I stood up to shake off the sleep that was overtaking me and leaned over the bed. I took Irma's hand and was startled to feel a faint squeeze. Then I saw her eyelids flutter. I turned to Dolores, grabbed her hand, and put it in Irma's. Again I saw her eyelids flicker though her eyes didn't quite open. She took another deep breath, let it out with a long whoosh, and then silence. I waited. Then Dolores saw it, the stillness. She looked up at Dave and then at me, then dropped her head on Irma's chest.

After a few minutes I got up to report that Irma had died. Brenda was still at the desk. She picked up to the phone to call the doctor; he would come in now, to sign the death certificate. She consulted hurriedly with Dolores; I stood next to her as she used the phone at the desk to call McCully's, the funeral home around the corner from the church. Back in Irma's room Dolores leaned over and kissed her on the forehead. Then we turned to leave. Dave and I linked arms with Dolores, holding her up as she stumbled down the hall.

Outside, it was still hot, the full moon blurred behind a scrim of haze. Dolores was out of breath, so we lingered for a moment in the parking lot, leaning into one another. I felt filled with wonder, marveling at the call that had brought me here. This cracked asphalt was holy ground. We three, the body of Christ. Blessed and broken, saints and sinners.

# CHAPTER 5

# HOLY MATRIMONY

It was my first wedding, and weeks before, I was already fretting about everything that might go wrong. When I'd admitted
my trepidations to my colleagues in ministry, they had regaled me
with stories of matrimonial mayhem: drunken groomsmen puking
or passing out, flower girls throwing fits, divorced parents at war
in the pews, no-show grooms, brides with second thoughts at the
eleventh hour. I'd brought on this razzing myself; clearly it was
part of my initiation into the clergy. Fortunately I hadn't told them
the whole truth. What they didn't know was that I had virtually no
personal experience of weddings.

I'd spent my twenties and thirties buoyed by the aspirations of
second-wave feminism. My closest friends and I had been stalwart
critics of the whole institution of marriage, and even as most of us
did succumb, one by one, not a single one of us had done the kind
of full-press wedding that was now again the norm. I'd never even
been one of a covey of bridesmaids clad in matching pastels, let
alone sashayed down the aisle in a wedding gown. Gary and I had
exchanged our vows in a no-frills ceremony at the DC courthouse,
so by the current inflated standards, I was barely even married.
I'd had maybe four hours of instruction on weddings in seminary:

one session of a pastoral care course, and a quick review of the ceremony itself in a liturgy class. So I felt filled with foreboding, even as I told myself my apprehensions were outsized.

Crystal, the bride-to-be, had barraged Constance with phone calls even before I had arrived, insistent on pinning me down for her wedding. She and her intended had set a late-summer date with the interim pastor; now Crystal feared that they'd be left at the altar with no pastor. Once I had reassured Crystal that of course I'd take on the wedding, she had assumed a businesslike, even brusque, approach to dispatching any remaining details. In a way it was a relief that she wasn't the dewy-eyed bride of central casting, and yet even I felt a little taken aback by her complete lack of sentimentality. When it came to weddings, she'd been there and done that—married with children, and now ready to do it again. She and Jimmy already had a life together, and a son to add to her two; he also had a teen-age daughter from an earlier relationship.

So this probably wasn't a typical wedding for the Saints, but it seemed like an ideal starter wedding for me. Crystal and Jimmy had planned a simple ceremony with a few friends, relatives, and their four children in attendance. The Saints' own music director, Marie, was enlisted to play the piano. The event was scheduled for a Saturday afternoon, and we'd probably wrap it up in under an hour. How hard could it be?

It was another brutally hot day, the sky white with Baltimore's August haze. In the dim sanctuary the air conditioners were laboring away, and overhead fans churned the warm air. Crisp linens lay on the altar, and silk paraments caught the light. The big Bible was open to 1 Corinthians 13, and I had tucked my sermon under the back cover. Charlene, newly appointed wedding coordinator, was dressed for the occasion in a flower-printed blouse and black linen pants, her reddish blond curls soft around her round face. As I reviewed the bulletin yet again, she patrolled the entrances, looking up and down the street for sightings of the bridal party. At fifteen minutes to zero hour, I was getting uneasy, but Charlene assured me, "Pastor, weddings never start on time." Thank God someone knew what we were doing. I pulled on my freshly laundered alb and set the stole around my neck.

I was relieved to see Marie coming down the aisle, wearing musicians' black with a wide-brimmed black straw hat set over her neat cornrows. She had been the music director at Saints and Sinners for some twenty years, and her brisk competence steadied me as we did a quick review of the service. She pulled out a sheaf of music and began to play as I lit the candles.

A few guests had begun to straggle in, staking out places in the pews with bulletins or purses and then wandering out again. At two o'clock, when we were supposed to start, I went over to the piano to touch Marie's shoulder and let her know we were still waiting for the key players. She nodded and stood up to pull more music out of the bench, setting down the lid with a bang.

I retreated to the sacristy and paced back and forth as the minutes ticked away. At two fifteen I stuck my head out the sacristy door. Marie was soldiering away at the keys, twisting around every few minutes to look for me. Her face was grim, her gaze set in the glare locally known as the "stink-eye." I ducked behind the door to get out of her sight lines.

I remembered the counsel of colleagues about starting a wedding on time, no matter what. This accorded with my own conviction that tardiness should have been one of the seven deadly sins, so I had been prepared to enforce punctuality on this occasion. But I could not quite see how to proceed without the bride and groom.

Last night's rehearsal had not gone all that well. Jimmy was barely speaking to me, clearly not mollified by my total capitulation in the matter of the video recording. A week earlier, in our last wedding preparation appointment, he had asked about getting the cameras set up. Lamentably, I had not thought to mention that no photography was allowed until after the service. On his own part, Jimmy was incredulous (and then outraged) that a pastor would contravene the documentation of such a significant life passage. As he explained through clenched teeth, making the video was practically the whole point. For years, he told me, he had imagined revisiting the day again and again, with an instant replay of his wedding always at hand.

"Jimmy, c'mon," I had pleaded. "Someone in our faces with a camera right during the service? That makes it into a performance. The whole idea is being fully present to the moment."

Jimmy had paused for a long beat, scowling. Then he stood up and declared that either the cameras would roll or the wedding was off, pending the location of a more suitable venue. Crystal, who had remained impassive through this exchange, now met my eyes and shrugged slightly. "It's his first wedding," she explained charitably. She followed him as he stalked out. After a few days' tense standoff, I had caved.

Last night's rehearsal had started late. Crystal fumed as the rest of us waited for Jimmy. When he finally arrived, I whisked them into my study for a quick consult. Crystal brushed me aside and began to berate, with an impressive barrage of complaints, the groom-to-be. As I remember, the conversation went something like:

"Dammit, do I have to do everything? What did you do with the license? How's my mother supposed to get the kids fed if you can't get here on time? Where are my cigarettes?"

With his trademark economy of expression, Jimmy replied to each question, "Shut up." The volume increased with each repetition, and his face got redder until it was an alarming purplish hue.

"Stop it, both of you," I ordered. "Let's get this rehearsal going or we'll be here all night."

Later that night, I mused that a more adept pastor might have called a halt to the rehearsal and sat them down for some emergency pastoral counseling. But somehow, I doubted that I would have been able to pull it off, even if I'd had the presence of mind to insist on it.

So far, my attempts at counseling had not unfolded quite as I'd envisioned. Before my first meeting with Crystal and Jimmy, I'd ordered a half dozen copies of *Preparing for Marriage*, the workbook recommended by my pastoral-care professor. They'd be my practice run, and then I'd have the books on hand for future couples. The workbook took the couple through everything from family history to retirement planning, with chapters covering sex, money, conflict resolution, and more. It even had homework, tear-out sheets that the prospective bride and groom were supposed to fill out independently, then compare their answers and discuss. I'd been impressed by its thoroughness when we reviewed it in class. My own marriage preparation had been limited to an appearance at the courthouse to apply for a license. The clerk barely looked up as we presented our identification. She typed in our names, collected the $2 fee, and then pushed the license across the counter to us. In retrospect, I could have benefited from some counseling myself. Then again, one reason we'd done it that way was to avoid the kind of counseling I was now inflicting on Jimmy and Crystal.

I hadn't done any damage that I knew of, but I wasn't sure our premarital counseling sessions had done them any good either. The personality inventories and genograms, the indices of intimacy and reflections on the future: all were as remote and alien to them as NASCAR and biker bars were to me. And it wasn't just the apparatus. *Preparing for Marriage*, I soon realized, was riddled with assumptions that had no application here. For one thing, it was directed to young couples getting married for the first time. Then there was the chapter devoted to the decision to have children; that ship had sailed. Dutifully trying to stay with the playbook, I'd asked if they planned to have more. "Jesus," Jimmy muttered, while Crystal rolled her eyes. I took that for a no. The book offered sound instruction on household budgets and financial planning, but this had limited utility for people who had to apply considerable ingenuity to get from one paycheck to the next.

Crystal sat through the appointed counseling sessions with barely concealed scorn. Jimmy, though, applied himself doggedly to the process, clinging to any talisman against marital disaster. When we met for the first session, he'd asked me, "How long have you been married?" He seemed reassured to know it had been twenty-four years. But my track record as a pastor did not inspire confidence. Every time we met, he asked me how many couples had gotten divorced after being married on my watch. "None!" I replied each time, adding, in the spirit of full disclosure, "but you know, Jimmy, I'm a new pastor, and you two will be the first I've married."

As for weddings themselves, my ignorance was vast. As a young teenager I had pored over *Seventeen* with its advice on what to wear as a wedding guest, and its instruction on the duties of bridesmaids anointed to attend their older sisters or cousins. But alas, I had no female relatives of marriageable age, and my one older cousin, Brian, had gotten married in a disappointingly tasteful Episcopalian ceremony. A maid of honor and a lone bridesmaid clad in yellow A-line shifts were the only attendants, and the bride wore a simple white dress, not even an actual wedding gown. A string quartet provided the accompaniment as she came down the aisle. Needless to say, they weren't playing "Here Comes the Bride."

By the time I graduated from high school in 1968, Holden Caulfield had displaced Prince Charming as the hero of my romantic fantasies. As for weddings, what now leapt to my mind was not the glamorous displays of *Bride* magazine but the iconic ending of *The Graduate*, where Benjamin Braddock rescued Elaine Robinson at the altar, barred the doors of the church with a purloined processional cross, and scooped her and her voluminous bridal gown onto the getaway bus. In the spring of my sophomore year of college, abortion was legalized in New York State, and the next December, *Ms.* magazine published its first issue. When a few of my friends did marry within a couple of years after we graduated from college, they wore wildflowers in their hair and dresses they had sewn themselves.

I myself had proved unequal to the rigors of even such minimalist nuptials. Gary and I had agreed to keep it simple, but almost immediately we hit a vexing complication in the matter of venue. I'd imagined a small gathering at my childhood Lutheran church. Gary was Catholic. "Lapsed," I would have said, but as it turned out, not so lapsed that he could abide the services of a Lutheran pastor. On my own part, I'd dreaded the prospect of planning even a small ceremony. I was racing to meet a publication deadline for my first book, and was loath to give up writing time for guest lists, menu planning, dress shopping, and the rest of it. And neither of us relished the prospect of submitting to premarital counseling. So with minimal discussion we had soon downsized to eloping in place. We picked a date and made an appointment to get married at the DC courthouse, telling no one ahead of time. Gary wore a dark business suit, while I donned a flowered skirt and a tweed jacket in shades of muted lavender, peach, and brown. We blended right in with other morning commuters as we walked through the city to the courthouse, where we stood before the judge to exchange our promises in the appointed ten minutes. After, we celebrated with a sumptuous lunch at a French restaurant and then took the subway to work, to let our colleagues make what they would of our shiny new wedding bands.

Fortunately, Charlene was a wellspring of wedding lore, well versed in the ways of blue-collar Baltimore and filled with a quiet passion for getting these things done properly. If the ushers asked where to seat the friends of the groom, or the father of the bride needed instruction on how to crook his arm for his daughter; should the best man fumble with the pins on his boutonniere or a bridesmaid's hem come down ten minutes before the service, Charlene, I felt sure, would know what to do. Upon accepting the invitation to serve as wedding coordinator, she had assembled a repurposed makeup case supplied with all the essentials, from breath mints and bobby pins (two sizes) to tissues and tampons. We were *equipped*.

But even Charlene couldn't produce a storybook wedding without the bride and groom.

At two twenty Charlene triumphantly reported that the bride had arrived. One down, one to go.

At two thirty I peered out onto the street. A limo rolled up with the groom on board. But then, it pulled away from the curb and turned down the block. Now what? I retreated to my study via the back entrance, leaving Marie still stranded at the piano.

At two thirty-five Charlene hunted me down, stray curls pasted to her damp forehead, to report that the limo had returned and decanted the groom. Lights, camera, action!

I peeked into the sanctuary, only to discover that the guests had gone missing.

"Charlene!" I hissed. "Where is everyone?"

"Pastor?" she said, a puzzled look on her face.

"The *guests*! Where did they go?"

"Er, well, they're outside."

"Huh? What are they doing there?"

"They're *smoking*, pastor," she said. "I'll go round them up." She looked out the door. "Oops, well, when Crystal's ready. She's out there too, just lighting up."

At two forty-five, the principals were finally in place. I signaled Marie to get ready to switch to the wedding march. She shot me a haggard look and muttered, "About time."

Jimmy stood next to the piano, sweating profusely. He was arrayed in a tight white satin matador's suit with fitted sleeves, gold brocade stretched over his chest, knee-length pants, white stockings, and buckled shoes. And I couldn't help but notice that this garment featured—could it be?—a codpiece. Jimmy's friends greeted his entrance with hoots and cheers. In response, he set both hands around the codpiece and hefted it up and down, presumably resetting the contents. The crowd yelled in approbation.

Marie struck a few loud chords to quell the disturbance and then launched into the wedding march. At the back of the church, Charlene flung open the doors, and Crystal swayed down the aisle, accompanied by appreciative whistles and catcalls. Her low-cut gown fit smoothly over her slim figure. Her honey-blond hair was piled on her head, with a few tendrils escaping to frame her delicate features. Her five-year-old son, Charley, clung to one hand, with his seven-year-old brother on her other side, carefully carrying a pillow with the rings secured by a loop. Jimmy pulled out a handkerchief, mopped his face, and finger-combed his mustache into place. As Crystal reached him, he looked her up and down and let out a low whistle.

The little crowd settled into the pews as I read the familiar words of 1 Corinthians 13, "Love bears all things, believes all things, hopes all things, endures all things. Love never ends. . . . Faith, hope, love, these three—but the greatest of these is love." My sermon challenged those heady sentiments with a dose of realism from the marriage service itself. Right before the vows are exchanged, the Lutheran rite declares, "Because of sin, our age-old rebellion, the gladness of marriage can be overcast and the gift of the family can become a burden." As we all knew, I went on, many marriages fail. Our lives are littered with broken promises and shattered dreams—and lit by hope and second chances. Then I stood in front of Crystal and Jimmy as they faced each other and clasped hands. My own voice shook a little as I whispered the phrases of the wedding vows and Jimmy and Crystal repeated them in turn. They'd both known the anger and grief of failed relationships; now they had the courage to try again, to promise themselves to each other "until death parts us." They'd endured much hardship, from brushes with the law to the daily struggle to make ends meet; now they pledged to share their lives "in joy and in sorrow."

Jimmy jerked his head at the ring-bearer, who stepped forward obediently. He fumbled with Crystal's ring, then pushed it down her finger. She worked his ring over his knuckles.

"Those whom God has joined together let no one separate."

It wasn't in the marriage rite anymore, but Jimmy desperately wanted to hear me say it. So I concluded, "I now pronounce you husband and wife. I present to you . . . Mr. and Mrs. James Edward Swanson!"

Jimmy grabbed Crystal and bent her over backwards for a passionate kiss. The crowd clapped and cheered. He let her go to brush a hand over his eyes. Crystal smiled tolerantly and took his arm. On cue Marie played the recessional salute, and they sauntered down the aisle.

The church cleared out quickly. As the little crowd dispersed, I overheard one guest mutter, "They'll never make it."

Marie was bustling around at the front, putting away the sheets of music scattered on the piano. "They got their money's worth," she observed. I hung up my vestments and unbuttoned my collar. Charlene and I roved around the church, putting out the candles, picking up bulletins, scraping a wad of gum off a pew, and sweeping up the cigarette butts on the sidewalk. Finally I sank into a pew.

"Well!" I said, sighing with relief. "That was nice, once we got going, wasn't it?"

Charlene regarded me silently.

"Wasn't it?"

"I don't think it was very romantic." Her face brightened as she went on, "The church was full for my wedding! I had six bridesmaids in apricot chiffon, and Jerry wore a tux with an apricot cummerbund. And my dress was so pretty—crystal beads sewn all around the bodice, and gathered in the back with a four-foot train."

She paused and looked at me curiously. "Pastor, what was your wedding like?"

"Er . . . small." I added hastily, "Intimate."

We did one last round of the church, turning off lights, locking doors. Charlene declined my offer of a glass of wine.

I went through the hall to the parsonage, kicked off my shoes, and flung myself onto the couch. The dire prediction of the departing guest echoed in my head, and I wondered myself how this marriage would fare. But then I decided I was going to be hopeful for them. Shadow followed me into the kitchen, where I poured a glass of wine. I turned to her and raised it in a silent toast for Crystal and Jimmy, or maybe it was a prayer.

# CHAPTER 6

# SLOUCHING TOWARDS
# BETHLEHEM

My first Noel with the Saints! I was curious to learn how they kept Christmas, and excited too as I calculated the potential for outreach. I'd been deflated when the crowds had melted away the Sunday after Easter. But Christmas loomed with promise. The conventional wisdom held that the late service on Christmas Eve was the biggest opportunity of the year, the service most likely to draw young adults back to church. Starting in October I'd been barraged with ads flacking seasonal banners, postcards for bulk mailing, and glossy brochures to lure newcomers. In our weekly Bible study, clergy colleagues traded tips about how to appeal to seekers without outraging the regulars.

I'd already been warned to keep my hands off Winter Wonderland. In the profile that the Saints had prepared for the call process, they got to list three things they did not want to see changed. Winter Wonderland had made the list—all the more notable, since it had been started by the very pastor vilified for her activist ministry to homeless people and her passion for rescue dogs. She'd since been virtually exiled from congregational memory. Yet Winter Wonderland had survived the erasure. Obviously, the Saints loved it, whatever it was.

When I'd asked council about Christmas Eve, they told me that the pastor traditionally hosted a reception in the manse between the two evening services. I was a little surprised that these reserved Saints would invite themselves to the manse, but touched that they cherished this tradition. I imagined a big fresh tree in front of the fireplace, stockings hung on the mantel, and the Saints milling around under the crystal chandeliers. At the same time, I couldn't suppress a sinking feeling. How was I supposed to play the gracious hostess in between leading two Christmas Eve services? I needed a wife, not just any wife, but the good old-fashioned kind, a pastor's wife who would cheerfully decorate (and clean!) the house, bake holiday treats, iron the linens, lay the table, and welcome guests. But I'd have to make do without her. Gary and Zoe would help, and Georgia told me that the Saints would show up with cookies and snacks to supplement whatever we set out.

I hate Christmas.

I'd felt a rush of relief when I finally admitted it to myself, sometime in the late 1980s, and soon enough discovered I wasn't alone. There were a lot of us out there, cringing at the carols, dreading the shopping, and trying in vain to hunker down until the whole thing was over.

I could still get sucked into the quicksand of nostalgia as colorful lights twinkled in the early dark and glittering decorations brightened the drabness of late fall. Growing up, I'd loved our family rituals: decorating cookies, shaping marzipan, watching Dad anoint his fruitcakes with whiskey. Christmas Eve was the high point, with cousins and aunts and uncles arriving with stacks of packages. After a festive dinner, Santa Claus would make an appearance, played by a ruddy-faced and rotund neighbor who'd bang on our front door, shaking his jingle bells and pulling small gifts out of his pack to delight the little kids.

Even then, though, I'd been attuned to the hazards of the season, the lurking tensions that might erupt to hijack Christmas.

The Christmas tree was a flash point, reliably accompanied by angry words and tears as it wobbled in the stand or when one of us stepped on a delicate ornament. Christmas morning began in much anticipated delight but often ended in tears, as we kids squabbled over something, or one of us knocked over the floodlights Dad had set up so he could record the occasion on camera.

The balance of Christmas—from delight to woe—had shifted inexorably over the years until I'd arrived at full-bore loathing. Even as a college student, I'd started to feel burdened by it, as final papers and exams pressed up against Christmas shopping and holiday plans. By my late twenties, I'd accounted Christmas as one more item on the long ledger of women's oppression. As I remembered childhood Christmases, my nostalgia was tinged with chagrin and a new appreciation for what those occasions had cost my mother. She'd been the one to buy and wrap all those packages, and in time to get some of them mailed too, so that my sixteen cousins and twelve aunts and uncles would get them by Christmas. And that wasn't even counting the presents from Santa that would appear under the tree. The dozens of cookies, the table set with carefully ironed damask, the Christmas Eve dinner, and Christmas morning cranberry bread—she'd done it all.

As a mother myself, I'd enjoyed a brief interlude of bliss. For the first couple of years, Christmas had come as a magical surprise for Mike. But by the time he was three or four, he'd fallen from the Eden of timeless delight to the overwrought expectation that kept him—and me—ricocheting between breathless anticipation and massive meltdowns. It wasn't just the extra work, though there was plenty of that. Worse, I could never seem to resist the claims of Hallmark Christmas, the pressure to come up with delicious meals, platters of homemade cookies and sweets, piles of presents, stockings stuffed with treats, a glittering tree—the stage set for celebrations unmarred by frayed tempers or simmering resentments. Needless to say, I wasn't able to pull it off, and yet I couldn't seem to let it go either. Christmas seemed like the final exam of the year, and every year I failed.

I longed to abolish Christmas forever, but that was a forlorn fantasy from the start. And now that I was a pastor, I could hardly own up to my inner Grinch, let alone undertake a campaign to steal Christmas. Instead, I resolved to ride the wave, to appeal to the nostalgia and sentimentality that washed over the land like a tsunami. Marketers had made it into a science, freely plundering the repertoire supplied by Currier & Ives, Norman Rockwell, and Charles Dickens, not to speak of Coke and Kodak. On wrapping paper, greeting cards, and department-store displays were images of stained-glass windows glowing in the snow, carolers serenading their neighbors on picturesque city streets, beaming families gathered around bountiful feasts. God bless us, every one! The appeal to a simpler time, unsullied by loss or regret, was a cheap but highly effective ploy to pry open hearts and wallets.

At the same time, it also spoke to some deeper longing, a heartfelt desire for real community, for enduring love, for lives of meaning and purpose. Most of the young adults in our neighborhood didn't expect to find those things in church. But many had grown up in church, and at Christmas some might feel the tug of memory that could draw them back to church, if only for Christmas Eve.

"Come Home for Christmas!" I contemplated my creation with satisfaction, a slogan that used the emotional resonance of "home" to welcome people to church. I hoped it would touch those who'd left church behind, even as it also might appeal to young adults who'd left their first families and might not feel quite at home yet in their new lives. And so a marketing campaign was born.

I pored over websites and brochures of outreach materials, rapidly discarding anything that involved rosy-cheeked cherubs, beaming choristers, or soft-focus Nativity scenes. I didn't want anything too churchy, either; I doubted the Gen Xers around us would warm to images of pipe organs or altars set with candles and greens. After much deliberation I chose a photograph of a wicker wreath covered with cranberries hung on a white door—simple yet festive and, I hoped, subliminally invoking fantasies of the heartwarming scenes that awaited behind that door.

I'd enlisted three or four of the Saints as a Christmas outreach team. Georgia had come over one day with a glossy 5x7 postcard from a megachurch in the city, their outreach for Christmas. I looked at it and then handed it back, shaking my head with regret. Bulk mailing on this scale would set us back a couple of thousand dollars at least. Instead we settled on hangers and matching postcards; we'd place the door hangers ourselves and hand out the postcards to members so they could use them to invite neighbors and friends. I swallowed hard when I got to the checkout on the website; this stuff would cost us almost $600. When I proposed it to council, they went into default mode: heads down and gazes fixed on the table. That meant no. I prodded the president to get discussion and a vote.

A long silence ensued. Then Bruce, our forty-something deacon, said, "I don't know. That $600 could keep our doors open another month if it comes to that."

Martha countered, "No. We've got to do something. Let's try this."

Around the table, council members looked furtively at one another when Chuck called for the vote. Martha's hand shot up, followed by a couple of others, and then everyone but Bruce had voted yes. He hesitated for a long moment, then let out a heavy sigh and raised his hand to make it unanimous. Game on!

Four of us trudged around the neighborhood once the door hangers had arrived, covering fifteen blocks in each direction around the church. Every Sunday I exhorted members to take postcards to invite their neighbors for Christmas Eve. I pressed them on everyone who crossed my path: the cashier at the grocery store, the yoginis on mats near mine, dog walkers in the park. I advertised our Christmas Eve services in the weekly neighborhood throwaway and hung a banner on the gate in front of the manse.

I'd even schemed my way into the *Baltimore Sun*. In November I'd spotted an announcement for the annual Holiday Cookie Contest. Visions of free publicity danced through my head as I imagined walking away with the honors. Along with the recipe, entrants were invited to send a story about their contending cookie. My competitive instincts kicked into overdrive as I pored over the notebook where I clipped and annotated favorite recipes.

Aha, my cranberry shortbread: different, but not too far out of the box, studded with colorful dried cranberries and crystallized ginger. I sent off the recipe and waited. A few weeks later, I was jubilant when the food editor called to announce my victory. That week the cookies were featured on the front page of the food section, along with an article that identified me as the new pastor at Saints and Sinners. I'd also worked in a pitch for Christmas Eve, inviting readers to come to our services and stop by at the parsonage to sample the winning cookies.

The Saints were bemused to discover their pastor featured in the morning paper. Constance came in and gave me a wry smile, shaking her head at my antics. Chuck called to congratulate me and linked the article to our website. By Sunday the Saints had developed grave misgivings. Charlene worried that I'd have to produce dozens of cookies and someone else wondered out loud where all those people would park. Georgia looked skeptical; she met my eyes and gave a small shrug. I wasn't sure bribing the neighbors with cookies was going to pack the house, either, but it was worth a try.

The weekend after Thanksgiving was the rollout for Winter Wonderland. Gary and I escaped for our annual road trip to North Carolina, where both of my brothers and their families lived. As we drove back up I-95 on Sunday, I girded myself for the last lap; those weeks between Thanksgiving and Christmas were always a marathon. My mother was coming from New Jersey on the train, and our friend Ed would arrive also, traveling from Connecticut for this first Christmas after the death of Sue, his wife and my dear friend. Mike would blow through at some point, though there was no use trying to pin down the details; there was no telling when he'd arrive or who might be with him. I only hoped it wouldn't involve too many additional dogs. I'd be orchestrating this holiday on the home front while also working it—my first Christmas as a pastor!

We pulled up in front of the parsonage just as the congregation was launching into the last hymn. I stood outside the sanctuary and then stepped up to thank the retired pastor who had filled in for me. A few of the Saints did a double take, surprised to see me there, and then urged me to come downstairs to see the fellowship hall transformed into Winter Wonderland. Charlene hurried ahead of me to put on the lights.

I stood at the door, speechless for once. Strings of colored lights crisscrossed the room, blinking hectically. More than twenty artificial trees lined the room, decorated with more lights. On the stage were another five or six trees set around a huge plywood sleigh piled with wrapped packages and surrounded by drifts of white batting. A couple of battered reindeer stood nearby, dusted with glitter. In the center of the room, some tables were set up with paper placements for the lunches and dinners. Others were covered with secondhand goods on offer for the tag sale: coffee makers, waffle irons, plates and glasses, stacks of T-shirts and sweaters and jeans. Handmade crafts were displayed on yet more tables: knitted afghans, baby booties and bonnets, Christmas ornaments made of cotton balls and popsicle sticks and glitter. A throne flanked by wrapped packages had been readied for Santa. (That looked strangely familiar; when I took a closer look at the tall chair with its red plush seat and elaborated carved back, I realized it had been purloined from its usual place next to the altar.)

Next to me, Dave inhaled sharply and then breathed, "It's beautiful."

I stared at him, dumbfounded. Dave was buttoned up even by comparison to the rest of the Saints, and had heretofore betrayed no sign of any aesthetic sensibility. He sat unmoved through hymns that had half the congregation in tears. When I'd admired the antique white silk of our Easter altar cloth, hand embroidered with intricate fruits and flowers, he'd shrugged and agreed politely, "Nice." We both cared passionately about the liturgy, but while I loved its rhythms and range of feeling, Dave was concerned primarily to guard against any incursions of contemporary language. So who knew he'd go dewy-eyed at the sight of this Christmas extravaganza?

I almost laughed, then felt a rush of affection for him and for the Saints who'd worked so hard to assemble it all. It had taken most of three days, I knew, to get it all done. I walked around to admire the trees as the Saints beamed. Each had its own theme: one for the Ravens, decorated (of course) in black and purple and gold; another for the Orioles; one for the Fantasy Football league (Gary had signed up for that, in the spirit of taking one for the team). Another was laden with kitchen gadgets; another with lace and delicate white ornaments, with an angel clad in tulle on the top. I marveled at the Saints' zeal for Christmas and made a mental note to get my own tree purchased and decorated.

Years ago, I'd made a fragile peace with Christmas as I found my way back to church. At Mighty Fortress, I'd fallen under the spell of Advent, the four Sundays before Christmas, from that first Sunday when I had walked in to find the altar and pulpit draped in deep blue, with a large Advent wreath hanging from the vaulted ceiling. The wheel of greens was set with four thick white candles. Sitting in the silent church, I felt an almost subversive relief to find a refuge from Christmas. I loved the strangeness of Advent Scripture; in contrast to the relentless cheer of the run-up to Christmas outside church, these stories were harsh and brooding: John the Baptist ranting in the wilderness. Most of the Advent hymns were in somber minor keys, an antidote to the endless loops of canned carols I'd heard all week. While advertisers warned with growing urgency about the dwindling number of days until Christmas, in church the light increased each week, another candle on the wreath lit each Sunday. Hungry for more, I had found myself drawn to the candlelight Wednesday evening services too, accompanied by haunting chants. I couldn't officially resign from Christmas, not while Mike was small, but in the shelter of Advent I had found respite and refreshment.

In seminary, I'd gotten unexpected support for my bad attitude about Christmas. I'd learned that the Festival of the Incarnation (better known as Christmas) was a minor occasion on the Christian calendar, strictly speaking. Initially it had been conjured as a way to co-opt pagan celebrations of the winter solstice. Centuries later, the Victorians had taken it viral, and ever since, advertisers and retailers had labored to expand the territory of Christmas from December to Halloween and before. We were encouraged to nudge our congregants back to the liturgical calendar: a full observation of Advent, followed by twelve days of Christmas starting on December 25. (I loved the idea of reinstating Advent; not so much, the thought of extending Christmas until January 6.)

This was best undertaken by indirection, of course. Railing against the holiday season would only cast us as mean-spirited Scrooges. Instead, we could simply offer the alternative—strong Advent worship—and trust that some would respond, as I had, to its compelling rhythms. I had eagerly imagined myself planning midweek services and encouraging people to observe Advent at home. But there was no way I was going to get the Saints to embrace some amped-up version of Advent, not this year at least. I'd been ambushed by Winter Wonderland.

I swallowed my disappointment. I wasn't going to get the Advent I'd hoped for, but I was curious to experience this storied extravaganza for myself. By two o'clock on Friday, people began arriving to unload boxes of groceries and supplies. Soon a huge vat of tomato sauce was bubbling on the hulking eight-burner cast-iron stove, with pots of water standing by to heat for the spaghetti. On one end was a deep fryer for French fries; doused with gravy, those were a local favorite. Hot dogs, hamburger patties, stacks of yellow cheese, and loaves of white bread lined the counters. Coffee urns stood at the ready in the fellowship hall, surrounded by platters of baked goods. Every few minutes someone else came through the door with more cookies or fudge or cake to add to the bounty.

A little before opening time, I helped Martha haul the sandwich board out to the sidewalk, and soon people were streaming down the stairs. Martha shouted orders to George (working the grill) and to the team dishing up the spaghetti. Martha's husband, Bob, who had been a navy chef, hefted the huge pot of steaming water to one of the sinks, then dumped it all into a Goliath-sized colander. Others piled giant portions onto paper plates, doused the pasta with meat sauce, threw on a couple of slabs of garlic bread, and passed it to the servers. Meanwhile, at the tables people laughed and talked as they waited for their food, as kids raced around the hall and others got up to admire the trees or browse the sale tables.

At seven o'clock Martha pushed the last stragglers out the door, urging them to come back the next day for more. In the kitchen, Peggy (a kitchen crew stalwart) was slumped over the sink, her face pink from the hot dishwater. George looked exhausted as he put away the last of the food and pushed a dish rag over the counters. Constance untied her apron and added it to the pile of used dish towels and other aprons that Janey was taking home to wash for tomorrow.

On Saturday they did it all over again, opening with a breakfast menu at ten o'clock, a grill menu for lunch, and a chicken dinner with all the trimmings. By closing time the Ravens-themed crafts were sold out, and Santa looked haggard as he got up from his throne and unfastened his beard. Constance was gray with exhaustion, and even Martha was flagging as she announced it was time to go home and reminded everyone to show up on time tomorrow for one more round.

Winter Wonderland opened at noon on Sunday, and I figured I'd better make sure the second service ended promptly. I kept the sermon short and went briskly through the Communion liturgy; even so, half the congregation slipped out to get to their stations downstairs. The kitchen crew had bypassed church altogether, heading straight downstairs to peel mountains of potatoes and fire up the ovens for the roast beef dinner. I felt dismayed on their behalf when the attendance was lackluster. Some faithful regulars did finally arrive, people from a neighboring congregation who came every year for the roast beef. They ate heartily, exclaimed at the decorations, and wandered back into the kitchen to catch up with the Saints.

When we closed up at five, I stayed around to help clear the tables and then went back to collapse at the manse. I marveled at their stamina, even as I wondered if all the time and energy poured into this event was worth it. And I felt a bit resentful too, to see the effort they had spent on this—the same people who seemed listless, even enervated, when we needed volunteers for outreach or Sunday school or nursery duty. Still, I told myself, it was good to know they could summon the effort to pull off a big project.

A couple of days later, Constance was sitting at the council table looking over the ledger she kept in pencil. So what was the take? I asked. I knew that Winter Wonderland was by far the year's biggest fund-raiser. About average for the event, she told me. So, I persisted, how much was that?

Less than $3,000.

"Almost $3,000!" I announced the next Sunday, smiling and applauding as I thanked everyone for all their work. Meanwhile I resolved silently to make this thing more profitable, or sink it. What I didn't understand, then, was the pride they took in offering a festive event to the neighborhood, and the hope they clung to, against the evidence, that fund-raising could keep them afloat.

For the next couple of weeks the Saints seemed utterly depleted — and no wonder. The first Sunday after, we went downstairs to the fellowship hall to polish off the last of the stale cookies and cake, sitting around a couple of tables that had been cleared. Around us the remnants of Winter Wonderland lay abandoned, with old sheets thrown over what was left of the crafts and the secondhand goods. The menus were still tacked up on the bulletin board outside the kitchen. Someone plugged in the lights for a few of the trees, but the stage stayed dark and Santa's throne looked forlorn, a few shreds of beard stuck on the red velvet. (And there it all stayed until the third week in January, when the Saints finally roused themselves to put it all away.)

After church on the fourth Sunday of Advent, Martha marshaled a few people to decorate for Christmas. Eddy and Steve (Agatha's son and son-in-law) got up on ladders to drape artificial greens along the choir loft. Chuck brought a wooden manger up from the basement, trailing bits of straw; Martha directed him to put it in front of the church, and ordered Bob to find an extension cord to plug in the white lights along its edge. Others brought up half-size plaster figures to set around the manger—a couple of shepherds, one king, Mary and Joseph. I asked George to move the Advent candle stand out of the church and back into its storage closet; he frowned, then shrugged, when I explained Christmas Eve wasn't part of Advent. Betty and Lois put away the blue paraments and set out the ones for Christmas, white silk with a blue and gold manger in the center.

Countdown. On the morning of Christmas Eve, Martha and Constance and Charlene toted the poinsettias upstairs and arranged them around the altar, their red foliage glowing against the white silk and oak furnishings. Zoe arrived in the afternoon with bread and cheese and dips for the reception. I hustled our house guests through a quick dinner, then headed over to the church. Someone had retrieved the Advent candle stand out of the closet; there it was, four candles alight. Martha was herding the kids as they arrived; she'd told me they did an impromptu Christmas pageant, with our handful of Sunday school kids and any others who showed up in time. The choir was assembled downstairs in the music room, a cramped windowless space tucked under the stairs. Their voices wafted up the stairs; once again, Marie had wrought wonders with our singers, eight of them at full strength, but with surprising range and ability.

By seven o'clock the church was nearly full, with many unfamiliar faces. Chuck was serving as assisting minister, and I asked him to point out people he knew. He recognized many as the children and grandchildren of members—the extended family of the Saints. I saw Renee, my yoga teacher, dressed in a festive deep-red top and sitting with her husband, Scott. They lived in the neighborhood, so maybe we'd be seeing more of them. The other unfamiliar faces? "Chreesters," Chuck declared. When I looked puzzled, he explained, "Christmas and Easter people." So, a heartening turnout, though I couldn't claim to have bumped it up with our outreach campaign. Still, it hadn't been a total loss, at least not if you counted Renee and her husband (I did—I'd given her a postcard, after all). Anyway, the late service was more likely to draw young adults. And maybe some of them would show up for my prize-winning cookies!

The pageant proceeded with the predictable missteps and then some. Martha had muscled Alissa to narrate the Christmas story, a risky choice. Alissa was a precocious thirteen-year-old, a bright girl with an attitude. (In confirmation class she alternated between astute questions and adolescent disdain.) She read the story in a rapid monotone as Martha coached the actors from the sidelines; they wandered around the front, willing but befuddled. When we came to the climactic moment of Jesus' birth, Martha loudly cued one of the angels to wave a wand. Then Martha swooped in from the side, flinging a handful of glitter as she deposited the baby in the manger. I cringed at this Tinkerbell rendition of the incarnation. The whole point was that Jesus was born to a woman—and a young woman at that—born in a rush of water and blood, not borne to the manger in a whoosh of fairy dust. Well, I could edit the script next year and assemble a pageant that we could rehearse ahead of time. We went for the usual crowd-pleasing finale, dimming the lights in the sanctuary as people lit their little hand-held candles and sang "Silent Night." It was a cliché—shameless, even. But I fell for it every time myself; that night, as usual, I had to pinch myself to blink back sentimental tears.

I greeted people at the back door and then raced to the sacristy to throw off my alb and stole. Back at the manse, Zoe and Gary had laid out food for the reception. We had cocoa in the kitchen for the kids, and the mulled cider on the stove filled the house with the scent of oranges and cinnamon. In the kitchen, we'd opened a couple of bottles of wine. The Feldmans were adamantly opposed to alcohol, but this was my house, and I'd decided to claim the prerogative to serve it (discreetly and moderately). The first floor was already filled with people smiling and talking, their plates filled with bread and cheese and Christmas sweets. I'd set out dozens of slices of the cranberry shortbread on the table, along with a copy of the *Baltimore Sun* article. A few Saints called out to me with their approval of the cookies. A few others had discovered the contraband wine in the kitchen and lifted their plastic cups in a jaunty salute as I joined them. The choir lingered as the rest of the crowd dispersed. I felt high from more than the half-glass of wine I'd had, exhilarated by the Christmas Eve crowd, warmed to see the choir lingering to relax before the next service, and bursting with happiness to share it all with my mother and Ed, Mike, and his friend Ethan (who had brought a dog, but only one).

At nine thirty I got up reluctantly and straggled back to church with the choir. We were shorthanded for worship assistants, and I'd commandeered Mike to hand out bulletins. About twenty people, half of them newcomers, gathered in the candlelight. I'd met one of the young couples before; they were hoping to plan a wedding at the church. Two older couples had recently retired and moved back to the city, they told me afterwards. Two men were attending solo, and three others—probably in their thirties but looking worn out—let me know that they had recently moved into a sober house in the neighborhood, in recovery from drug abuse. At the door, everyone smiled and thanked me and wished me Merry Christmas. (I never saw any of them again, except for the couple who wanted to get married.)

Back at the manse, I unbuttoned my clerical collar, kicked off my shoes, and sank onto the couch with a mighty sigh of relief. We stayed up for another hour, laughing and talking, until Mom and Ed headed upstairs to bed, and Mike and Ethan started rearranging the couches to crash in the living room. I left them to it and went upstairs.

It was midnight. I looked out our bedroom window onto the empty street. Usually it was lined with cars; anyone coming back to the neighborhood after nine could expect a long search for a space. That night, whole blocks had only two or three cars at the curb. Where was everyone? Most of the new neighbors weren't churchgoers, and even if some of them had found their way to worship on Christmas Eve, they'd have been home by now. And I couldn't imagine that Christmas Eve was a big night for bars or restaurants, even if it was Saturday.

I had wanted to entice them to Saints and Sinners. "Come Home for Christmas," our invitations had cajoled, a message we had hoped would warm the hearts of young adults here for an internship or a graduate degree, or married with new babies. New to the city, most of them, maybe they would be longing for the community we could offer, a kind of substitute family. What I hadn't considered was that those twenty-somethings had families somewhere else, and those new babies were somebody's grandchildren. They had gone home for Christmas.

# CHAPTER 7

## SEEKER

Allison hunted me down before she had even moved into the neighborhood. She was scouting out the local congregations, and she called to let me know we'd made the cut, once she'd seen a woman pastor's name on our marquee. She stopped by to talk a few days later. It was late August, and a wall of humid air slammed me when I opened the door. Allison was probably in her early fifties, with short curls plastered to her head and her very pale skin slicked with sweat.

I fell on her with an enthusiasm that was just short of desperate, or at least I hoped it was; full-bore desperation was as much a buzz-kill at church as it was in speed dating. Once in a while we did have visitors who appeared at a Sunday service of their own volition (in contrast to the wayward relatives of members frogmarched into worship at Christmas and Easter), but this was the first time someone had actually sought me out.

In my study, she sat for a moment without speaking, looking intently at me with pale blue, almost gray, eyes. Then she told me she was moving from a Washington, DC, suburb, selling the house where she and her first husband had lived for many years. He had died about a year ago after a long physical and mental decline, the last of it spent in a nursing home. She'd met Roger along the way, and their friendship had warmed into more. They had married a couple of months ago and were planning to move soon to the row house he was fixing up nearby. He'd grown up in Baltimore, and houses were more affordable here. Besides, our neighborhood was close to I-95, convenient for his commute to DC.

I studied her curiously as she talked. Widowed, remarried, moving to a new city, Allison seemed plucky and resilient, ready to open up her life to second chances. And someone who had to be serious about church, if she was looking for a new congregation before she'd even moved into the neighborhood. Yet somehow I didn't figure her for a longtime member of some mainline congregation. Sure enough, she'd been in and out of several places: Methodist most recently, Episcopalian for a season (I was relieved to hear that—our worship closely tracked theirs), Presbyterian in there somewhere, or was it Baptist? She stopped at one point, fixed me with that intense look again, and said, "I seek to know and do God's will."

She was spiritual *and* religious—a combination seldom found in nature. People who called themselves "spiritual" usually appended "but not religious," meaning they felt some kind of tug to transcendence and a desire to find out more about it. Seekers, we sometimes called them, but whatever they were looking for, they didn't expect to find it in formal religious institutions. They'd either dumped church or never been there to start with. "Religious" was their epithet for what they'd rejected, meaning empty ritual, constricting creeds, rule-bound moralism.

Clergy spend much time and thought trying to parse the predilections of the "spiritual but not religious," also known as the SBNR (they'd earned their own acronym). Seekers are a tantalizing demographic, people avowedly open to exactly what we most value in church: a source of meaning and purpose, a place where all the deep questions are asked, a tradition that honors life's mystery and majesty. So they seem ripe for recruitment, and yet most prove maddeningly elusive. Since many of the pastors I knew thought of seekers as kindred souls, it was all the more frustrating to find our overtures rebuffed—even, we suspected, to be rejected as "religious" ourselves. Still, we regarded the SBNR as our mission field; these were our people, whether they knew it or not!

But how to enlist the Saints in this quest for the SBNR? I felt sure the Saints did not consider themselves spiritual, and I doubted they would call themselves religious either. As far as they were concerned, God was in charge, and it wasn't their place to have any opinions about what he was doing. Their job was to shut up and show up. A month into my ministry—an early earnest phase— I'd herded the Saints into small groups to inquire, "Why do you go to church?" To a person, they had replied, "Because I always have."

That long faithfulness was alien to my own experience, and I sometimes wondered uneasily what they made of me, a pastor who'd spent twenty years out of church. I'd answered with appreciation for their steadfast practice of worship and their loyalty to this congregation; most had been there for years, some for a lifetime. But their dogged consistency was a problem as much as a virtue. Congregational life at Saints and Sinners marched in the lockstep of long habit, and from the beginning I had known I would somehow have to break that rhythm to reverse our steady decline.

So I'd pressed them a little, reminding them that our new neighbors were not like them. That was an understatement. The new neighbors were younger, affluent, college-educated, transient. Many were single; some were openly gay. And the married couples often didn't have children or had moved out of the neighborhood after their offspring reached school age, spurning the local schools the Saints and their kids had attended.

How would they talk about church to someone who hadn't always gone, who had left church or maybe never been there in the first place? After a long pause, Betty ventured, "Well, we're friendly. They'd like us if they came!" A couple of the Feldmans gave me icy glares. Marge crossed her arms over her chest, and Sally said in a hard voice, "Our doors are open. All they have to do is get out of bed on Sunday morning."

Allison continued, "Pastor Barbara, the sign out front says, 'A Warm Welcome Awaits You.'" She paused and raised her eyebrows. "So, will your congregation welcome me?" The fact was that the Saints were likely to consider her an alien, at least at first. I hesitated and then said that if she wanted to belong in this neighborhood, to connect with its deep history, getting to know our people would help her to do that. Saints and Sinners had been a landmark on this corner for over a century. Our presence had helped to anchor the neighborhood through the years when drug dealers threatened to take over. And now, when gentrification was changing South Baltimore again, Saints and Sinners could become common ground, a place where new neighbors met the old blue-collar neighbors, and longtime residents came to know and love the newcomers.

I'd gotten a little carried away as I delivered this pitch, and at the end of it I felt self-conscious. Saints and Sinners was a long way from being the kind of place I imagined, and the Saints themselves weren't exactly on board for it—not yet, at least. Still, a few of our members were longtime residents who had upheld the neighborhood tradition of knowing everyone on their blocks. But others were diffident, fearful, or outright hostile to the newcomers, and most had trouble even imagining the lives of anyone very different from themselves. The elusive subject of our tagline was all too telling. "A Warm Welcome Awaits You"—but who would offer it?

In mid-October I ran into Allison in the park; they had just moved in. That Sunday, she turned up at church. I held my breath as she headed down the aisle and settled into Edna's pew, right behind Constance and George. Then Edna herself appeared and started to make her way down the aisle, neatly dressed in black pants and a pink top printed with cat pictures, her beehive hairdo perfectly arranged. She started with surprise when she saw Allison had taken the seat that was Edna's own by long custom. She sat behind Allison, shooting me a meaningful look to make sure I'd registered her forbearance. But her sacrifice was in vain. Allison called me that afternoon with a crisp review. The sermon got high marks; the music, meh; the liturgy, more formal than she liked. She didn't come back to worship the next week, or the next, and I figured we'd lost her.

Oddly, though, she maintained a lively interest in what I was doing with the Saints, to the point where I had begun to feel under surveillance. She kept me apprised of her findings as she scrutinized our signage, evaluated our landscaping (such as it was), and reproached me for the weeds coming up between the cracks on the sidewalk. The newsletter commanded her rapt attention. She was my most avid reader (for all I knew, the only one). Every month, as soon as the *Herald Angel* hit her mailbox, Allison combed through it and called me up with commentary, corrections, and suggestions for improvement. She even came back for worship once in December.

Still, how was I to know she would turn up at a Lenten supper? Yes, I had flacked the event in the *Herald* and concluded with our congregational tagline, "A Warm Welcome Awaits You Here!" A rash claim, admittedly, but one unlikely to be tested. The occasional newcomers who came to check us out typically did so at the Sunday service, with timing calculated to minimize contact. Visitors would show up just as the crucifer was lofting the cross down the center aisle; ducking in behind the procession, they'd then secure seats in the back, in order to facilitate a rapid retreat. If a visitor were to return, it ordinarily took several more weeks before the newcomer could be cajoled to join us for coffee downstairs. It was an operation requiring the utmost delicacy. Too subdued a welcome, and we would be deemed cold and unfriendly. Too fulsome, and the visitor would flee like a hart, never to be seen again. But attending a congregational supper as a newcomer—that was nearly unheard of. So how was I to know that Allison would forsake her position as friendly critic at the margins, to fling herself into our midst in the fellowship hall, of all places?

Supper was almost ready, with the big soup pots set on warmers next to bowls of salad. I had drawn coffee duty, a task not without hazard. The electrical outlets on that side were notoriously unreliable. At times they shorted out with an ominous crackle, sending us hustling back to the kitchen to replace the burnt fuse. At other times they were deceptively quiescent, simply failing to work for reasons no one had been able to discern; thus we would be patiently awaiting coffee, only to discover the urn was stone cold. Attending to the electricity was not for the fainthearted, so I had enlisted Miriam as my wing man. Nearly eighty years old, she was tiny and frail but of a firm and fearless character. Constance hovered a few feet away, keeping an eye on both of us.

I gave a start as Miriam seized my arm and whispered in alarm, "Pastor, who's that?"

Across the hall I saw a woman with short curly hair edging into the room, clutching her purse. Flummoxed by this unexpected development, I didn't recognize her at first. Constance looked over and answered, "That's Allison, isn't it, Pastor? She came to church back in October, I want to say, and then again maybe a month or so ago. I believe she sat in Edna's pew."

Not for the first time, I marveled at her unerring recall. Constance never failed to note the names of visitors, and she was the acknowledged master of neighborhood history, with an unparalleled grasp of local genealogies. When you needed to know who was Edna's second cousin's hairdresser's uncle, Constance was your woman. So I was not surprised that she remembered Allison, *and* knew her name.

She added, "She's not from here."

The kiss of death. I countered, "Well, but she's a neighbor now. She and her husband moved here in September." I paused for effect and added, "Her husband's from here." I rarely had the opportunity to tell Constance anything she didn't already know. As she raised her eyebrows slightly, I felt a little surge of triumph.

Allison unbuttoned her coat and made her way over to the soups as the others shuffled to their usual seats. I held my breath. Now what? Seating in the fellowship hall was ordered according to an intricate geography of status and affiliation. The matriarch regnant and her entourage (devotees of the early service) occupied the front table close to the kitchen. The rival matriarch Agatha and her clan, the Feldmans, claimed their two tables on the far corner of the room, as far as you could get from Constance's table while still remaining in the fellowship hall. Four of the Feldmans were talented singers, the backbone of our small choir, so other choir members and their families sometimes sat with them too. A few other families staked out their own tables on territory that lay between the turfs of the matriarchs. Then there was the table of strays, as I had silently dubbed it. This table was the redoubt of those doubly disenfranchised, both bereft of extended family and not claimed by either matriarch. But it was also the terrain of a few sturdily independent members, among them Georgia, who maintained a studied neutrality. Gary and I were tacitly assigned to that table, though I circulated around to all the tables and upon occasion defiantly sat down at one of them.

Wandering haplessly onto this terrain, Allison was now marooned in a kind of no-man's-land. She hesitated and looked around the hall. No empty seats were available, except at the remaining table where no one was sitting. And naturally no one was leaping up to rescue her or make room for her at their table.

I tried to stifle my exasperation. I didn't find it easy myself, chatting up people I didn't know, but I'd learned how to do it in professional jobs that required it. Few others at Saints and Sinners, though, had the kinds of jobs that involved extended conversations with customers, and when they weren't at family gatherings, they hung out with long-familiar friends and neighbors. People weren't so much shunning Allison as overcome with shyness, or even trep- idation. What kind of person would show up at a church supper alone, without so much as a husband or sister or grand-baby in tow? I filled my own cardboard cup with soup and hurried over to join Allison with a feeling of sure and certain doom. No doubt I'd be hearing all about our defects in the hospitality department.

After the supper, we straggled upstairs to the parlor for a Lenten study on prayer. Allison followed along doggedly. Once people had settled into their chairs, I said, "So, let's go around and introduce ourselves!" This set off a flurry of consternation. "What are we supposed to do, Pastor?" Betty asked plaintively. Betty was a longtime member who lent a willing hand to everything from altar guild to pot scrubbing, but she sometimes had trouble shifting gears. "Say your name, Betty, first and last," I said. Thus instructed, the Saints began to comply. But when we arrived at George, he announced, in a rare show of defiance, "I'm not doing that. I already know everybody here, and everybody knows me." I cringed. Allison was sitting directly in front of him, across the little circle.

"I don't think so," I said through gritted teeth. I was practiced in waiting out silence after twenty years of teaching undergraduates, but I was no match for the Saints. After a few beats, I admitted defeat. "OK, everybody, that's George Ausdauer. Who's next?"

We limped through the hour until I sent them off with a closing prayer and retreated to the parsonage. As Shadow greeted me, I assured her sardonically, "'A warm welcome awaits you here!'" She tipped her head to one side, looking confused.

The next morning, Allison stalked into my study and demanded, "So what was that about?"

"I know, sorry! They take a little while to warm up, is all. Really, they're great people, when you get to know them. I hope you'll give us another chance."

"And what would I have to do to get to know them, Pastor Barb?"

I hadn't called myself "Barb" since high school—not that it mattered. But I felt a surge of annoyance anyway. I had a sermon to write and a draft of Sunday's bulletin to proofread. I'd just gotten a call from Dorothy; Gilbert was in the hospital, again. The toilet was running, again, in the tiny bathroom next to my study. I was sick of trying to woo Allison, sick of my own performances, sick of trying to fling myself across the abyss between my blue-collar congregation and newcomers like her. I was sick of Allison too, sick of her exacting expectations and her endless suggestions for my edification.

"Look," I said finally. "We aren't perfect, not even close. Finding a place here isn't easy, not because people don't like you and not because they don't want new people. They do. *We* do. But they just aren't used to dealing with anyone outside their own families."

More than that, I thought to myself, they don't know what to do with people like you, who've changed the place they knew and loved. The place where they grew up, and their parents before them. The place they held on to in bad years, as the neighborhood slid into drugs and crime. They'd banded together and driven out the dealers—only to be displaced, themselves, by young professionals and students and affluent retirees, people attracted to the low housing prices and the park and the safety they'd fought to reclaim. This place had been their home for generations. Now they were losing it, as they saw it, as the old neighbors moved out or died, and the row houses of South Baltimore filled up with strangers. "Anyway," I went on, "the fellowship hall is the last place you'd get to know anybody, honestly."

"So how come it's called the *fellowship* hall?" Allison persisted.

I said morosely, "Well, maybe we should call it the Death to Fellowship Hall."

She let out a startled whoop of laughter, and I started laughing too, until the tears ran down my face. But I felt guilty too, betraying the Saints with that snarky comment. I had the opportunity to repent at leisure. Every time I ran into Allison, she found some way to bring up the Death to Fellowship Hall. But she was no newcomer to congregational life. Hadn't she learned that fellowship halls were the last place a person would find—well, fellowship?

I had learned it the hard way myself. I still cringed to recall the first time I'd been scourged in a fellowship hall. I'd been out of church since high school when I'd first attended Mighty Fortress in 1980, during a yearlong stay in Washington, DC. I'd moved five times, changed jobs, become a mother, and buried my father before I finally decided, nine years later, to join that congregation. One warm spring day I was received into membership, "churched" again after nearly twenty years out. But I hardly knew anyone in the congregation. Now that I'd made it official, I resolved to change that.

The fellowship committee of Mighty Fortress had been hawking a pancake breakfast for weeks. I figured I could handle that.

By then I'd undergone a rigorous initiation into Washington social life on the nonprofit circuit. Gary and I both worked at the Smithsonian, and that meant required attendance at fund-raising galas, exhibit openings, and dinners feting donors. I learned to fake it at these pseudosocial events—circulating, smiling, and making small talk—but I hadn't learned to enjoy it. So, on the morning of the breakfast, my stomach knotted up as we stood for the closing hymn. But this was a congregation, after all—my congregation, now—not a roomful of potential donors. And it was a pancake breakfast, not a black-tie dinner. How hard could it be?

The fellowship hall was swarming with people greeting one another and finding places at the long tables set up with paper placemats and plastic forks and knives. I hesitated, then got in the line for food—a fatal tactical error. By the time I'd filled my plate with pancakes and picked up a Styrofoam cup of coffee, the tables were filled with people laughing and talking. I spotted one table with an empty seat, but when I worked my way over to it, I saw it had been staked out with a red purse. One table over, I tried to settle into one of the four empty chairs, only to be deterred by the well-groomed older woman at the other end: "Sorry, my family needs this whole table." Then I arrived at a table with three empty seats where a couple of kids were tipping syrup onto their pancakes under the supervision of a pleasant-looking older woman, probably their grandmother. Next to her a woman about my age looked up with a friendly smile. When I asked if I could join them, she replied, "Of course! Good to see you. Didn't you join a few weeks ago? Barbara, is it?" At last, a place at the table! And somehow, she even knew my name! I pulled up a chair and smeared butter on my pancakes.

Then Pastor Schmidt came over to the table, his plate piled high. "Grandpa, got enough pancakes?" one of the kids teased.

No! I was at the pastor's family's table!

It was like a bad dream, the kind I often had before some black-tie function. I felt like I'd blundered onto the head table at some prestigious event, glaringly out of place with the legitimate luminaries. A new member, rubbing shoulders with the pastor's family? How pushy was that? But no, it was even worse than that. Theirs was the only table with empty seats—the resort of the friendless.

Their warmth seemed very genuine, but I felt deflated all the same. They had to be nice, after all.

It took me weeks to recover from this first sortie on the fellowship hall, but I'd finally joined a church after twenty years, and I would not be denied. My fellow members were going to have to deal with me, whether they liked it or not. As I wrote in my journal, "Damn it, this is my church too!"

When we'd moved from DC to Wilmington in 1994, I knew I'd want to find another church, even as I dreaded being a newcomer again. Still, I'd survived it in Washington, all in the cause of getting a spiritual life. That mattered to me more and more, and I knew by then I couldn't do it by myself. I needed worship: the set-aside space of Sunday morning, the voices around me in congregational singing, the Bible read out loud, the reflection and challenge of the sermon, the depths sounded in prayer. Gradually I'd come to understand that church was about community too, life together as the body of Christ. If this meant that I had to suffer my fellow Christians along the way, so be it.

I figured I'd start at Fellowship Divine, a Lutheran church just a few miles from our new house. I found it just off the state highway, a low, contemporary building with a fluted octagonal roof and a sleek metal cross at its peak. Inside, the sanctuary's octagonal walls rose to a vaulted ceiling. Around a simple altar, padded chairs covered with rust-colored fabric were arranged in a wide semicircle. The floor was covered with shag carpet in a bilious pea-soup green. In contrast to the thin scattering of mostly elderly congregants in the pews at Mighty Fortress, this place was packed with people, most of them in family clusters. After the service I went home feeling uncertain but hopeful. I missed the elegant marble and wood of Mighty Fortress, its majestic pipe organ, Pastor Schmidt's probing sermons, and the reassuring familiarity of worshiping with people I knew, at least by sight. On the other hand, the people at Fellowship Divine were enthusiastic singers, and I had happily joined the altos singing harmony on some of the hymns. Pastor Pete's sermon was short, informal, and simple to a fault; but he seemed kind and thoughtful, and he'd greeted me warmly at the door and asked my name. Maybe there was a place for me here.

Fellowship Divine was growing apace, with another crop of new members standing up to join every few months. Resolving to be one of them, I signed up for the next session of orientation for prospective members, five weeks of meetings between the services. I had even braved coffee hour a few times, lingering hopefully near the clusters of people laughing and talking around the coffee urns and tables of homemade goodies. But no one seemed to notice me; worse, their eyes glanced over me briefly before they turned away. I became a three-time dropout of the new members' groups, and finally I had to admit that it wasn't only summer vacation and then soccer season that was keeping me away. The nasal electronic organ started to get on my nerves, and some Sundays the mystery of faith took second place to bemused wonderment that someone had actually chosen that hideous carpet. Still I persisted wanly—until the moment of truth came, on Christmas Eve.

After a tense standoff, I'd convinced Gary and Mike to go to church with me. It would be fun, I cajoled, with candlelight and carols, and afterwards we could each open one present. When this inducement failed, I declared icily that I'd go alone—*on Christmas Eve*. Gary capitulated under my glare. Mike wailed, and then howled in fresh outrage when I said he had to wear a collared shirt. Gary put on a crisp white dress shirt with a silk tie and a blue blazer, brushing aside my warning that he'd be the only guy in the room in a jacket and tie. I pulled on charcoal gray wool pants and a deep pink cashmere sweater set. I hustled them into the car so we'd get there early, to avoid the scrum for seats.

It turned out we were nearly the first to arrive, standing around awkwardly at the door as one of the ushers went to find the bulletins. The sanctuary was filled with poinsettias, and every inch of the place was draped with artificial garlands and blinking Christmas lights. I hesitated and then led Gary and Mike down the side aisle to seats a few rows from the front. I felt miserable, out of place again, and angry that I'd had to fight so hard to get Gary and Mike there. But they'd come, after all; so I resolved to ignore their scowls. It was Christmas Eve, time to let go of my resentment and make peace.

At the organ, the musician was arranging her hymnbooks and song sheets, dressed in one of the holiday sweaters that were an unofficial uniform here; hers was white with heavy red felt poinsettias appliqued on it, sprinkled with gold sequins. She turned around on the bench, smiling as she greeted us.

"Merry Christmas! How lovely to have you visiting tonight! Have you just moved into the neighborhood?"

I flushed with embarrassment, taken aback to be tagged as a complete newcomer. Mike turned his face up to me and said, bewildered, "Mom? I thought this was your church." Gary snickered.

I felt furious and humiliated; to my chagrin, I found myself blinking hard to hold back tears. This is the end, I vowed fiercely. When this wretched night is over, I'm out of here. I pasted on a smile and wished her Merry Christmas in return, hoping she hadn't heard Mike. She turned back to her music as the choir began to assemble and the room filled with people.

Later, I told myself I was overreacting. Fellowship Divine was a big congregation, after all, and for most of the service the musician faced away from it as she played the organ and piano and directed the choir. I couldn't blame her for not recognizing me. And naturally she did notice us that night, in the nearly empty room. But I couldn't help suspecting that I had also become more visible with Gary and Mike in tow—a churchgoing family instead of an unaccompanied woman.

Anyway, the truth was that this relationship was going nowhere. After six months, I hadn't met one person who seemed to want to know me. No one even knew my name, except for the pastor. I made a new year's resolution to find another church. At the end of January, Pastor Pete called and left a message, and then another a couple of weeks later. I listened stone-faced and deleted his messages without returning his calls. I felt a little guilty; it wasn't his fault that I hadn't gotten anywhere with the congregation. But I wasn't going back, and I didn't feel like talking about it. Petty as I knew it was, after months of feeling like an outcast, it felt good to dump them. I was done with those people—and their ugly rug too.

Allison proved to be more decisive than I had been, swift to commit or quit. A few weeks after the Lenten debacle, she let me know she was joining a United Church of Christ church on the other side of the neighborhood. It was a blue-collar congregation like ours, with a woman pastor.

A year later, she quit there and joined a nearby Presbyterian church with a faded rainbow banner hanging over the door.

A year after that, she dumped them for the neighborhood Methodist congregation.

I thought she might come back to Saints and Sinners on the rebound, sooner or later. I myself had returned to Fellowship Divine, and in a way I had never expected. I came back as a seminary student for my internship year; I became the first vicar they'd had and the first woman to preach from their pulpit. I'd taken the assignment with trepidation. Wouldn't they remember me, and resent my abrupt departure? It had been almost ten years, but many of the same people were still active members. Oddly, no one seemed to recognize me; even stranger, I did not recognize any of them. Pastor Pete had not forgotten me, and no doubt he had not forgotten my abrupt exit either; but he received me graciously and helped to form me as the pastor I would become. So who knew? They had been too happily enclosed in their own circles of friendship to welcome or even to see a stranger. But then again, maybe I had been too quick to judge them — too prickly and defensive, and too hungry for acceptance, to practice the patience and forbearance that life together requires.

Allison maintained her keen interest in the *Herald Angel*, and from time to time she consulted me about some matter of faith and life. She and Roger came to some of our events. She never did come to worship again, though. I felt a little exasperated that she wouldn't give us another chance, even as I also admired her persistence in searching for what would satisfy her hungry heart. Seekers are a hard crowd, I consoled myself. It had taken me years to commit.

But now I was the pastor, and I had to figure out some way to bridge the divide between the Saints and the seekers around us. How could I get my dear but dour members to open their hearts to these perplexing newcomers? How could I get those newcomers to let go of their expectations long enough to let the Saints touch their own hearts? Already I was feeling the tug of another anxious question: How long could I keep doing this before these Saints and seekers broke my heart?

# CHAPTER 8

# BUILDING CODE

A church is not a building, as my clergy colleagues and I never tire of reminding one another. But our congregations are in buildings, and those buildings consume prodigious amounts of time, energy, and money. Routine maintenance is death by a thousand cuts: a leaky tap in the kitchen, a running toilet, a loose carpet. Then there are the body blows of big-ticket repairs: a roof replacement, a boiler failure, a crumbling stone façade, or a weight-bearing beam riddled by termites. Even one of those calamities can be the knock-out punch for a congregation already struggling to pay the bills.

When a fire destroyed the building of a Methodist church in the city, not a few of us found ourselves feeling a certain transgressive envy. Of course we didn't wish a devastating fire on anyone, least of all our own congregations. Still, it was a measure of our scourge by property that the smoldering ruins of a church building could spark fantasies of liberation: the chance to start again, to become a church not shackled to a building, with a hefty insurance check to fund that dream. When the Methodists opted to use their one-million-dollar windfall to restore the old building brick by brick, we shook our heads.

Almost all of our city congregations bore the telltale signs of being overwhelmed by their buildings: flaking paint, brick in need of pointing, water stains, scuffed floors, and broken sidewalks. Yet, shabby as they might be, these buildings were beloved, and woe betide the pastor who attempted to meddle with them. In small churches especially, I had been warned, buildings are a flash point for conflict between pastor and congregation. I resolved to stay clear of property matters.

Who knew that I'd become obsessed with property projects and embroiled in controversies over everything from paint colors to building use? That I'd ride roughshod over congregational governance to get my way on renovation? That I'd become a general contractor by default? That in the final reckoning I would count property improvements as the single unambiguous accomplishment of my ministry among the Saints?

The Saints loved their traditional worship space, and I shared their appreciation for the classic beauty of its stained glass and elaborately carved oak. It was the best-cared-for space in the building, though even here there were signs of neglect. The dull-red carpet was worn and threadbare in places. Near the entrance a scorch mark in the shape of an iron bore witness to a misbegotten effort to clean up spilled candle wax. Over the altar, Jesus was missing a couple of fingers on his right hand.

I soon assumed a proprietary attitude toward the building (so much for minding my own business). Because I had been a museum curator years ago, I was highly attuned to concerns that were lost on the Saints (and, to be fair, to most other people outside the arcane world of collectors). My fellow curators had educated me about the ravages of dust, rust, mold, rot, and more. We handled objects with white gloves to protect them from the oil on our hands and fiercely defended our collections against heat, light, and damp. So I cringed to see the sterling silver baptismal shell black with tarnish, and the antique silk veil for the chalice splattered with wax. Still, I cautioned myself not to criticize.

My noninterference policy came undone by the scourging of the oak doors in the sacristy. The Saints used them to post notices and schedules, irrevocably damaging the wood with cellophane tape and punctures from thumbtacks. When I caught Martha in the act, a notice in one hand and a thumbtack poised to stab, I pleaded with her to cease and desist, and convinced the rest of the altar guild to do the same. Buoyed by this victory, I vowed to eradicate the tape wantonly applied throughout the building. I drafted a newsletter article instructing the Saints on the destructive properties of adhesive, along with guidelines for how and where to affix notices to the wall or other surfaces.

But when I presented it for proofreading, Ellen called me into her office and asked, "Pastor, do you really want to publish this?" Ellen was the part-time administrative assistant I had convinced council to hire, and she had proved an invaluable asset. A longtime member of the local Catholic parish, she knew congregational life from the inside; she had also grown up in the neighborhood. More than once, she had saved me from some inadvertent transgression on local practices or mores, and I'd come to rely on her experience and wisdom. But this time I'd countered that the Saints loved their building, and surely they would appreciate my efforts to preserve it. She let a long silence develop while maintaining an expression of studied neutrality. "Oh, all right," I conceded grumpily. I settled for removing taped notices whenever they appeared on wooden surfaces. The Saints promptly put them back again.

That was small stuff anyway, I consoled myself, as I took inventory of the place.

Downstairs, the fellowship hall was shabby but serviceable. Its old linoleum tiles were warped in places, and the flowered valances on the windows stiff with dust. The chairs and tables were old but in good repair. The kitchen hadn't been updated for probably a half century, but its many cupboards had been repainted more recently than that, and the labels taped on each of them corresponded to what was inside—no mean organizational feat, since they held prodigious amounts of plates, glasses, cups and saucers, pitchers, platters, sugar bowls and creamers, vases, and more.

The Sunday school room was dismal with peeling paint and a stained and worn gray carpet. The walls were covered with warped bulletin boards displaying tattered projects from Sunday schools of yesteryear. It was a large airy room looking out onto the manse's back garden, but the tall windows were streaked with grime. The low bookcases that served as room dividers were stuffed with papers and plastic bags. Even so, the room was still usable, with space for a couple of tables and plenty of child-sized chairs for the Sunday school classes.

Across the hall was a room completely overtaken by clutter. The Saints universally referred to it as the Scout room, though it had been years since any Scouts had met there. Barely visible behind the piles was a fireplace set off by beautiful stonework. Two over-sized chairs and a couch covered in faded pale-blue velour wafted mildew. Against one wall, a huge glass-fronted cabinet held tro-phies from the glory days of the Saints and Sinners' softball team, along with plaques commemorating the achievements of Boy Scouts who were now probably grandfathers. Tables were cov-ered with paintings on black velvet, candles, lamps with broken bases and tattered shades, rolls of butcher paper, and more.

The worst clutter lurked in the nether regions under the church and manse. The large basement comprised a warren of closets and rooms. Partially refinished with dull red and white linoleum and knotty-pine paneling, this area had once housed the overflow from the Sunday school. In the early 1960s, some two hundred kids had been enrolled; an old photograph showed them lined up in front of the church. An interior shot from that era showed the basement set up with room dividers and furnished with handmade wooden altars, the same ones that were now jammed up against the walls and piled with stuff. Part of the room was cordoned off with sawhorses and string with a hand-lettered sign reading, "Do not remove anything from this area." It was a kind of makeshift workshop, filled with tools that belonged to George, kept here for church repairs but also likely as overflow from his home workshop. Behind one door, I discovered what looked like a machine shop, its workbench and equipment covered with thick dust and cobwebs.

I dubbed the basement the "heart of darkness."

The clutter haunted me like some evil presence. I saw it as a reg-ister of decline, a visible sign of the congregation's loss of energy and their tenacious hold on the artifacts of their imagined past.

Spaces that were no longer used had steadily filled with junk, like the weeds and broken glass that filled the vacant lots in the neighborhood. Like those vacant lots, the unused rooms of our building continued to attract new deposits of clutter with a magnetic force. Members reluctant to throw out their own discards brought them to the church. We even had the occasional anonymous donation to deal with: bags of discarded clothing left on the church steps like baskets of abandoned kittens. But our biggest challenge came from within. Constance and George were inveterate savers, loath to relinquish anything in their custody, and inveterate collectors too, who rarely encountered an object that did not suggest some rich promise of future use. They added steadily to the accumulations and fiercely resisted any efforts to get rid of anything.

Still, I'd been encouraged to discover that I wasn't the only one upset by the accumulations. A few months after I'd arrived, I had called together a small group to set goals for the congregation. Cleaning up the place was high on the list. I even had two confederates who were eager to take on the job and, unlike me, eminently qualified for it. Georgia was an interior decorator with a notebook full of the names of contractors and wholesale suppliers. Charlene was a tireless and resourceful organizer, a clutter-buster extraordinaire, and Jerry, her husband, had a truck.

But months went by, and then a year; I couldn't figure out how to get traction on the project. The sheer volume of it was overwhelming; I felt defeated in advance as I considered what it would take to move the mountains. Georgia and Charlene were ready to tackle the stuff but leery of taking responsibility for proclaiming what counted as junk. Any cleanup effort also meant challenging Constance and George. I was the pastor, and council members were the congregation's elected leaders, but everyone knew that Constance ran the place. She actively supported me on some fronts and put up with me on others, but nothing happened at Saints and Sinners without her tacit consent. The Saints knew from long experience that she would resist any assaults on the collections. A few people grumbled about George's expanding workshop in the basement, but since he did most of the repairs around the church, no one was ready to criticize him openly either.

Thus were we stymied, once again. Too much of the decision making at Saints and Sinners operated just like this; we'd consider a change and then reject it on the basis that it might upset someone. I had resolved to break through the deadly stasis. To that end, I'd drawn on my long experience in academic administration—years of wrangling professors, a veritable Olympics of management. I'd supplemented that with training workshops in congregational leadership. Council had proved impervious to it all, and my attempts at one-on-one conversations fared no better. So much for persuasion, negotiation, and consensus building. It was time for direct action.

We resorted to covert operations. I cleared out a large closet packed from floor to ceiling with plastic grocery bags, filling eight giant trash bags. When no one noticed that, I went to the basement and hauled out a very large cardboard box sagging with damp. George promptly rescued it. I should have known I'd never get away with it; I already knew that George opposed the disposal of any kind of container, including used envelopes. Alerted to my depredations, Constance and George began to move some items from the basement to the council room for safekeeping. Georgia and I shifted operations to the parlor, where we purloined the tattered artificial ficus trees, sneaking them out under cover of darkness to discard them in the trash cans in her back alley.

Next, Charlene volunteered to clear out the basement. I felt a twinge of conscience, sending her alone into the heart of darkness, but she insisted that she loved a challenge. She descended downstairs for hours at a time, emerging filthy and triumphant. George hovered nearby, his face stormy, but she avoided the areas he had cordoned off, and he put up with her incursions elsewhere. When she'd finished, I marveled at the neat shelving and labeled bins, and exulted as Jerry hauled off loads of discards. We scored another victory by securing the perimeter against further flea-market backwash. Any unsold merchandise, we declared, would either be reclaimed by the donor or taken to Goodwill. The Saints agreed without a whimper. After the next flea market, Jerry rolled up with his truck and Charlene supervised the removal of the remnants.

Still, we'd barely made a dent in the massive accumulation. The Sunday school room was still a mess, and the Scout room was filled halfway to the ceiling. I didn't want to admit defeat, but I felt my energy and enthusiasm waning—until a missed opportunity galvanized me into action.

"Pastor, Pastor!" I looked up to see Betty hurrying down the side aisle to the sacristy, where I was hanging up my alb and stole after the first service. "A visitor! She's here with her little boy looking for the Sunday school!" I felt as excited as Betty about the prospect of a new recruit. We were hanging on to the Sunday school by our fingernails. Jill and her cousin Cheryl, both from the Feldman clan, took charge of the three elementary school kids, while the two or three preschoolers were supervised (sort of) by Louise, an overworked woman in her forties. The curriculum was makeshift. I had ordered colorful workbooks and teachers' guides with lesson plans. A few weeks later, I discovered the unused workbooks and teachers' guides stuffed into a cubbyhole. When I asked about it, Jill and Cheryl shrugged and answered that they were looking them over (in the cubbyhole?), while Louise rejected them outright, complaining the lessons were too complicated. Most weeks, the older kids did some craft project, while Louise watched the younger kids play with the battered toys scattered around the room.

I had let it slide; I was in no position to try to get our current teachers to do anything they didn't want to do. I had tried and failed to recruit others to help them; when they couldn't make it, Sunday school didn't happen. The Saints often averred, "We need more young families!" The same people, it turned out, were loath to spend time taking care of what they deemed "other people's kids."

In the narthex I found a woman dressed in a blue blazer over a striped top, her blond hair in a sleek cut. Elizabeth, she told me, and the little boy holding her hand was Ben. He looked to be five or six years old, with an adorable headful of brown curls. They had just moved into the house right around the corner, and she was looking for a Sunday school for Ben. As we chatted, I imagined her and Ben in the pews, and Ben joining the little group of kids who came up for the children's sermon. And maybe Elizabeth could spell the others for an occasional stint in the Sunday school room.

I hustled them through the shabby hall down the stairs to the Sunday school room. Louise was sitting on the floor with two four-year-old boys who were driving toy trucks. At a small table, Jill watched three kids gluing cotton balls on construction paper sheep. They all looked up as we came in, staring at the strangers. I prompted Jill, "So, can Ben join you guys this morning? Let's pull up another chair for him!" Jill looked a little startled but then smiled shyly and said, "Sure, come on over."

I turned to Elizabeth, who was gripping Ben's hand with a dismayed look on her face. "Ah, no, that's OK, maybe another time." She turned and headed out the door, pulling Ben along with her. After that, I saw her occasionally around the neighborhood, but she avoided my phone calls and invitations to come back to church. I didn't know for sure that the shabby and cluttered room had been the deal breaker. Maybe she was looking for a place with more kids, divided up by age into more classes. Maybe Jill and Louise didn't look like what she expected of Sunday school teachers. Maybe I hadn't measured up to what she expected in a pastor. Still, when I remembered the look on her face as she fled, I was seized with renewed determination to clean up the place.

Georgia and Charlene brightened when I announced it was time for us to make an official declaration of war on clutter. They'd be the project managers, we decided, and I'd take on the job of wrangling the congregation. We sealed the pact with high fives. We resolved to clean up the Sunday school room and reclaim the Scout room. Then we'd have an inviting room for children, and the choir could move out of their cramped windowless space under the stairs. We got estimates for painting and recarpeting both rooms, and council approved in principle. But the expenditure was more than they could approve for an item that was not in the annual budget, so we had to go to a congregational vote.

At the meeting, the gathered Saints were guarded. Constance and George protested about spending the money, with hearty assent from a couple of other fiscal conservatives from the early service. What was the point, anyway, since we had hardly any kids in Sunday school, and no one was using the Scout room? And where was this money supposed to come from? Yes, the congregation did have a hefty savings account, but that was for a rainy day. Then a few people spoke up to defend the project. We had to take care of our building. And the new neighbors had expensive tastes; they wouldn't settle for good enough. The fiscal conservatives fell back to challenging the estimates. Weren't there cheaper options? Georgia looked grim. She had already warned me that she didn't want to be second-guessed by amateurs. We'd had gotten her professional advice for free, along with deep trade discounts on high-quality carpet.

Then Marge stood up. (As Agatha's older daughter, she was first in the line of succession for matriarch of the Feldman family and already taking on some of the heavy lifting.) No question, the place was a mess, she said all too emphatically. But carpet in the Sunday school room? The kids would spill juice and scatter crumbs, step on crayons and dribble glue. Anyone could see that tile was a better choice. Sally nodded in agreement as her sister spoke (the Feldmans always took a united stand in congregational disputes). Georgia huffed in exasperation next to me. Of course tile was better, she muttered in my ear, but that would cost twice as much.

I had expected some objections, but I was caught off guard by this unlikely alliance. The dueling matriarchs rarely agreed on anything, and I'd been counting on the Feldmans to go along with the proposal, if only out of resentment for the early service contingent and their tightfisted ways. But now it appeared they also resented Georgia, and probably me too, for proposing a big project with no prior consultation with one of them. I scanned the room, silently counting votes. We could go down in flames, or win by such a close vote that the rancor would linger long after the smell of new paint had dissipated. I hastily proposed an amendment. Could we vote to approve the budgeted amount, on the condition that the project would be delayed until we could get estimates for tile? We wanted to get the rooms ready in time for the start of

Sunday school in September. Georgia scowled and declared that she was done with getting estimates. Looking grimly triumphant, Marge and Sally volunteered to take it on. The Great Tile Compromise passed with only a few nays.

The clock was running out on the estimates for painting and carpet. Georgia, Charlene, and I started poring over paint chips so we would be ready to go as soon as the tile contretemps was settled. A couple of weeks later, Marge and Sally produced the tile samples and estimates. I tried to ignore the tension in the Sunday school room as they laid them out on the floor. Georgia was visibly annoyed, and Charlene kept darting nervous glances at me and the Feldman sisters. Constance and George had abandoned their posts in the council room to monitor the proceedings.

I was wistful as we looked over the samples, especially the one that was soft gray flecked with blue. As we sat on child-sized chairs in the shabby room, I imagined the dirty carpet replaced by gleaming tile. Just as Georgia had predicted, it was much more expensive. Still, I mused out loud, it would look lovely, and of course it would be more practical too. Should we go back to the congregation and ask for more money? Georgia snorted and Charlene looked incredulous; even Marge and Sally seemed taken aback.

Constance burst out, "We don't have the money. This isn't like *your* church."

*My* church? She meant Good Shepherd in Wilmington, where she and George had attended my ordination two years ago. The reception afterwards had been in the newly constructed fellowship hall, with its fresh paint, tiled floor, and custom window treatments. I felt as if I'd been sucker punched. Ordinarily Constance treated me with careful deference and what I had thought was mild affection. Now, it seemed she regarded me as an alien, even an interloper. *My* church? Georgia gave me a sidelong glance, while Charlene and George looked fixedly at the floor, assuming the default position for a flummoxed Saint. "This is my church," I said, stiffly.

A long tense silence followed. I fought back tears of hurt and anger. This project was long overdue, and we were going to get it done one way or other. We defaulted to the original plans for carpet as Marge and Sally offered one final round of admonitions about what the kids are going to do to it.

I exulted as we moved the project to the next stages. Georgia started lining up painters and carpet installers. Charlene commandeered Jerry and his truck, and they hauled off the mildewed couch and chairs. Jerry and a couple of burly friends moved the storage cabinets out of the Scout room and into the basement, where Charlene had excavated some space. But by early August I realized uneasily that I had become the project manager. I was spending hours on meetings with contractors that Georgia had called for estimates, reviewing plans, scheduling the work. We would not have the rooms ready for the opening of Sunday school, as we'd hoped, but very soon we would be moving into two clean, refreshed, and well-organized rooms.

But then the project stalled at a critical juncture. The painters were scheduled to arrive in ten days, and we had to do a massive cleanup to get the rooms ready. Charlene firmly declined; she could not do anymore. Georgia declared that she was going out of town for a week and, anyway, the work was too heavy. I wasn't sure if they were just burned out, or had lost their nerve for a project that had stirred up more than dust in the congregation. I didn't have the heart to ask, either. They had already done so much, and maybe it had been unrealistic to think we could pull this off by ourselves. But now, somehow, this had become my project—and my problem.

I needed reinforcements, but who? I ran through the short list of able-bodied members. The Feldmans were the mother lode, with a half dozen men and women with the skills and muscle to do it, but their disagreement about the tile probably meant they would decline the invitation to help. I couldn't ask Constance and George to help execute a project they were barely tolerating. Martha and Bob were away for the week. So that left me, and I couldn't do it myself. I would have to call off the painters and abort the mission.

Then the Lord provided! Mike (my son) called with a request on behalf of his buddy Kyle, who had had a run-in with the law and been sentenced to forty hours of community service. He had let it slide, and now his court date was looming. Did I have anything he could do? I gave a victory fist pump in my study as I described the project. Mike offered to come along to help. For the next five days, we whaled away at the clutter as an August heat wave slammed the city. As fans churned the saturated air, the guys dismantled bulletin boards, unscrewed light fixtures, moved furniture, and took down faded pictures, releasing clouds of dust. While they did the heavy lifting and climbed up and down ladders, I sorted through the cupboards and shelves, throwing out bottles of hardened glue, stacks of brittle and fading construction paper, torn costumes, and rotting fabric remnants.

George hovered around the edges, casting a dour eye on the proceedings, but he lent his drill to Mike and Kyle and gave a forbearing shrug when they promptly lost two of the bits in the rubble. He watched without protesting as we hauled dozens of bulging garbage bags out to the alley. Constance stayed clear, sequestered upstairs in the council room; I worried she was too angry to even look at me. But when I went up to my study, I found a bag of fresh tomatoes and cucumbers that she had brought for me. They were dead set against the project, and yet they put up with it, and me. I admired their ability to suffer my depredations without holding a grudge.

When the rooms were cleared, I sent off Mike and Kyle with thanks and a sigh of relief. The next day the painters arrived, followed by the carpet installers. I was on the job as general contractor, running back and forth to let workers in, monitoring their progress, getting checks cut. In between, I cobbled together the Sunday sermon, proofread the bulletin, and prayed none of the Saints would land in the emergency room or the hospital.

At last it was finished. The dust had settled, and the smell of new paint and fresh carpet filled the air. In the Sunday school room, the muted blue-green was a perfect complement for the terra-cotta on one accent wall; the colors were echoed in the carpet (a blend of teal, gray, and dull red, to disguise the spills). In the Scout room—no, the *former* Scout room—a deeper blue-green set off the granite fireplace. Georgia and Charlene came over to inspect the results. Georgia took a long appraising look around the rooms, then nodded with satisfaction. Charlene grinned and hugged me hard. I couldn't wait for the unveiling. Once people saw the rooms, I enthused, they'd be thrilled, and it would all be worth it. Charlene's smile dimmed, and Georgia said, her mouth set, "We'll see."

On Sunday morning I urged the congregation to come downstairs after worship to see the refreshed rooms and to help move furniture. As they filed downstairs after the last hymn, I followed close behind, eager to see their faces when they saw the results. Charlene and Georgia stood off to one side, looking guarded. One by one, the Saints came into the Sunday school room, bearing small tables and chairs, maneuvering book shelves, replacing the child-sized altars against the walls. No one said anything, and their faces were unreadable.

Filled with dismay, I scanned the room and then went over to Danny, Jill's husband. They had recently married, making him one of the Feldmans, but I thought maybe he would talk. "So, what do you think?" I asked, trying for a brightly casual tone.

He set down the chairs he was carrying and regarded the room thoughtfully.

"Um, who picked the colors?" His tone was carefully neutral.

Marge snorted, "It looks like a circus tent!" She was still mad about the tile, it seemed. In earshot of this review, Georgia looked grim, and Charlene flushed unhappily.

If anyone else in the congregation had an opinion about the makeover, I never heard it. I felt blindsided and furious—stung by this reception myself, and upset on behalf of Charlene and Georgia. They were both resigned. Charlene shrugged; this is just how the people were at Saints and Sinners. "Germans," Georgia pronounced. Stolid, and sparing of praise.

The next morning, I felt disconsolate. Had the whole project been a waste, or worse? Then the phone rang. A young mother who had recently moved into the neighborhood was calling to ask if we had a room that could be used for a parents-and-toddlers group. I startled her with a burst of laughter before inviting her to come over. When she saw the Sunday school room, she exclaimed, "This is perfect! We'd love to meet here if we could." A couple of weeks later, I went downstairs to greet five moms and their kids, romping around the room and, yes, crumbling cookies on the carpet.

Charlene painted a new sign for the door of the former Scout room, black letters on a soft green background, "Singers of Saints and Sinners." The next Sunday, the choir moved out of its cramped space next to the furnace room into the spacious new music room. At first, they complained—even Zoe and Marie, usually my loyal allies in the cause of change. The carpet dulled the sound, and their voices sounded thinner in the big high-ceilinged room. Besides, they missed the intimacy of their old room. For an awful moment, I was afraid they were going to insist on moving back into their windowless lair. Then Marie rallied and declared they'd get used to the new room. The next Sunday, a newcomer appeared who wanted to join the choir. They could not have squeezed another person into the old room, but now there was plenty of space to add another chair and music stand. The week after that, another new member joined the choir.

A church is not a building, but its building tells the congregation's story: its history, its commitments, its morale and spirit. A church is not a building, but its building can become a graveyard of abandoned ministries and lost dreams. Getting rid of clutter and refreshing our rooms had created space for new activity and new people. The Saints had been resentful, opposed, or indifferent to this project, most of them. But with a few determined people, we had gotten the job done. I felt emboldened and filled with renewed resolve. We were going to drag the Saints into new life, like it or not.

# CHAPTER 9

# SHATTERED

We were on the cusp of Lent, my second at Saints and Sinners. Snow had kept most of the congregation home that Sunday. But today the sun was melting the snow on the roof and sending water rushing down the rain spout, a good portent. It was Fat Tuesday (Mardi Gras in French), and here in Baltimore that meant pancake suppers — a traditional way to use up fats in preparation for Lenten austerity. The Saints had been bustling around all day, unloading groceries, setting up tables, frying bacon and sausage.

Downstairs in the kitchen, pitchers of pancake batter stood next to the huge stove with its cast-iron griddle. A dozen waffle irons were stationed along the counters, strung together with extension cords. In the fellowship hall, vats of cherry, peach, and apple topping were arrayed on warming trays. The tables were set with paper placemats and decorated with red and yellow plastic flowers in terra-cotta colored plastic pots. Once we were under way with an event involving food, I was strictly forbidden to go into the kitchen, along with anyone else who had not been anointed to the kitchen crew. So I took up my post in the fellowship hall, where I had been deputed to work the front of the house.

Our first customers showed up right at the stroke of four. These were our stalwarts from Rock of Ages, a Lutheran congregation a couple of miles away, who loyally attended all our events (as we did theirs). They got their tickets at the door, then claimed their usual seats at the front table. I brought over tea and coffee, then sat down while they ate to catch up on the latest news. Dispatching our pancakes, they headed off for St. Ann's, the neighborhood Catholic parish, for the next stop on their traditional Fat Tuesday tour.

I took advantage of the sudden lull to put in my own order. Last year—my first pancake supper—I had thrown the kitchen crew into consternation by requesting a half order. No one had done such a thing in living memory, and they were upset to think I'd pay full price for half the pancakes. And anyway, who would spurn a full plate of their pancakes? This year I'd taken the precaution of skipping lunch, determined to acquit myself honorably with the full stack. I scooped on cherry topping and started forking down the pancakes. But just a little more than halfway through, I was already starting to flag. When a crowd of customers arrived, I set my plate aside for later.

I was settling them at the tables when Arlene came hurrying through the door—by herself, I saw with surprise. She was one of a large extended family, and normally she was accompanied by some of them, or at least one or two of her fellow singers in the choir. She scuttled across the room, her head down, and said to me in a low, urgent voice, "Pastor, something terrible has happened." I studied her face with alarm. Arlene was the oldest sister in her family, steady and competent, the one others turned to when a teenager went off the rails or a husband strayed. "It's Janey's husband, Jim." Janey was a linchpin of the choir with her fine soprano voice, and a stalwart contributor to bake sales, cleanup efforts, and more. Jim didn't come to church, but I had met him at our events and saw him regularly at the post office, where he had worked for some forty years.

I strained to make out the story between Arlene's sobs. I hadn't realized that Jim had a sister, Beth, who had moved away years ago, and not just out of the neighborhood. She'd followed her husband, Kevin (not from here), to upstate New York, where he had a good job as an engineer. Their daughter, Jenny, was fourteen years old. Jim wasn't estranged from his sister—not exactly—and Janey did try to keep in touch with her sister-in-law and niece. But they might as well have relocated to another planet. Jim had never been on a train, let alone braved an airplane, and had ventured out of the state only rarely.

Now all three of them had been found dead. Kevin had strangled Beth, and their daughter too, then killed himself.

I reached for Arlene, who half collapsed against me. "Oh no, oh my God," I murmured over and over, holding her tightly as her whole body heaved with sobs. I bit my lip hard to stop my own trembling.

She straightened up and fumbled for a tissue.

"So, does anyone have any idea . . . ?"

"Pastor, I don't know, they said he was acting strange, getting into trouble at work. And she was trying to leave him, I guess, take their daughter and get away. Jim didn't know about any of it, though, until the police called.

"Anyway. The family is bringing them home, and Janey wants to know, can you do the funerals? She didn't want to ask you herself, Jim isn't a member, they grew up Catholic, but nobody else in the family goes to church, and . . ."

"Of course I'll do it," I said, reeling away from the idea of it, *no no no*.

"Oh, Pastor, she'll be so relieved. They're at the funeral home now, making the arrangements. Should I tell them, oh, I just don't think I can take any more today, or . . ."

*Pastor.* I was their pastor. I could do this. "No, I'll call her."

She let out a jagged sigh. "I was supposed to help clean up. Pastor, can you tell Martha I had to go home?" I threw an arm around her and led her out the side door.

A cluster of new arrivals came down the stairs. I blew my nose and tried to wipe the shock off my face. Say hello, thank people for coming, agree the weather has been awful. Smile, nod, shake hands. I felt numb and oddly removed as my mind filled with nightmare images: a desperate man holding on to what he would not let go of; the terror of breath squeezed off; the police officers breaking open the door to find the bodies. I willed myself to stay in the room, do the work in front of me; time enough later to enter the horror. Smile, nod, shake hands. In the next lull, I sat down to my pancakes, sized up what was left of the stack, and put down my plastic fork again.

Suddenly there was a tremendous crash of broken glass, followed by a blast of cold air. A young woman at the next table screamed, and in the high chair next to her, her son started wailing. Others startled and jumped up, pushing chairs back from the tables. One of the big windows had shattered, spraying shards of glass across the room, along with a drift of icy snow. I looked up to see the window blocked with a wall of snow four feet deep.

Martha yelled from the kitchen door, "Anybody hurt? Pastor, do we need 911?"

"Everybody's OK. Keep the kids away from the glass. Somebody, sweep it up. And we've got to cover that window."

The rest of the kitchen crew was clustered behind Martha, craning around her to see what's happening. She wheeled around. "Back to your stations! We've got customers out there. Bob, get this mess off the floor." He straightened up and gave her an ironic salute, then grabbed a push broom and shoved a big plastic trash can over to the spill of snow and glass.

George came over to stand beside me, surveying the damages. "Here we go again," he said dolefully.

"What? So this has happened before?"

"Well, yeah, a few times." I felt a rush of impatience. This happened before, and nobody fixed it? But then he explained that when there was heavy snow on the steep slate roof, then sudden warming, the snow could suddenly pitch off the roof into the narrow space between the fellowship hall and the parsonage. When the avalanche hit the brick wall of the manse, it ricocheted across the gap to smash into the windows. I didn't quite get the physics, but that was beside the point right now. "OK, we've got to get that window covered and fast. Can you figure that out? I'll go outside and clear out the snow."

I ran upstairs to the manse, pulled on boots and a jacket, grabbed a shovel, and floundered outside into the narrow space crammed with snow. Al and two other men were standing there sizing up the mountain of snow. I pushed past them and jammed the shovel into the pile, almost eye level in front of me, then pivoted and dumped the snow behind me. I drove the shovel into the pile again; it sliced through the icy snow with a satisfying crunch. The horror of Arlene's news began to fade away in the rhythm of this physical work—loading the shovel with snow, flexing my knees to lift the weight, then heaving it behind me. Soon I was sweating from the exertion. I felt exhilarated by the cold air and the sweet ache of well-used muscles. I stopped to push my hair out of my eyes and was suddenly aware of my audience. The men were standing there looking bemused. I wondered belatedly if I had insulted them by taking on the heavy lifting myself, but with the snow piled up there was only room for one person, and I had the shovel. Besides, they were at least fifteen years older than I was. Bob flashed me a smile and said, "Pastor, want me to take over for you there?"

"Nah, thanks, I got it."

"You're stronger than you look, girl." He shook his head in admiration.

Just as I had finished clearing the window, George appeared with a half sheet of plywood, a hammer, and a box of black trash bags. I backed out, and Bob and George started boarding up the broken window.

Back in the fellowship hall, I pulled off my jacket and soaked gloves. Someone had cranked up the heat, and blasts of hot air mingled with the cold leaking around the plywood. George came back inside, set a ladder up against the window and taped up black plastic. A few customers had left hastily when the snow and glass crashed into the hall, and a few newcomers were grousing about the draft, but we had managed to keep the supper going. Suddenly ravenous, I looked for my plate. I sloshed some warm syrup on the pancakes and devoured them.

Martha was stripping down the tables around me, though it was only six thirty. We advertised we were open until seven, I reminded her. "Around here we eat at five o'clock," she countered. At the ticket table, Miriam and Constance were adding up the receipts. Miriam thumbed through the bills carefully and then reported, "Over $400! That's good, isn't it, Pastor?"

Constance shook her head. "We won't clear half that." As the financial secretary, Constance watched every penny and regularly delivered dour assessments of our financial situation. In an effort to counter her reflexive pessimism, I maintained an attitude so resolutely upbeat that it bordered on delusional. So I turned to Miriam and chirped, "Yes, so great to see people coming here and having a good time! And everyone loves our pancakes!" Miriam beamed as Constance took the stack of bills from her and started counting, maintaining her signature poker face.

In the kitchen, Martha whirled around, putting away food. Peggy stood over the industrial-size sinks and rinsed the last of the utensils, her round face red over the steaming rinse water. Bob wiped the counters, shoulders slumped with fatigue. A couple of the men sat at the long stainless-steel worktable, hunched over the last of the lukewarm coffee.

Ten minutes before seven, the door clanged open and a crowd of people spilled into the hall, five couples with kids in tow, stomping their boots, unzipping jackets, pulling off scarves. I recognized two of the women from the parents-and-toddlers group that met here on Mondays, and went over to greet them. Meanwhile, Martha was glowering from the kitchen door. She had left one table set up, so I ushered them over there, and then hastened to the kitchen to plead for pancakes.

Martha crossed her arms over her chest. "Pastor, it's almost seven o'clock. Supper is over."

"Well, but we said we're open until seven, and we don't want to send these people home hungry." I felt a pang of guilt. Martha was a woman of prodigious energy, but even she was sagging with exhaustion after hours on her feet.

She scowled, then sighed, "OK, we can do it." She pushed her hair back under a hairnet and turned to the kitchen crew. "What are you standing around for? We've got people to feed!"

I went over to the table to chat up the clientele. They talked and laughed, complimented the pancakes, scrounged around the remnants at the bake sale table for dessert, and lingered on and on. From the kitchen door Martha threw me meaningful looks that morphed into glares and then the dreaded stink-eye. I was getting exasperated with them myself. Couldn't they see the supper was over? Martha brought out the push broom and advanced. They held their ground, lifting up their feet amiably so she could sweep under them. She set the broom against the wall with a bang, cleared off their plates and cups, wiped off the tablecloth, and took the table down. With that, they finally cleared out.

After we had finished the rest of the cleanup, I staggered out the door. Back at the parsonage, I unbuttoned my collar and peeled off my clergy shirt. Under the hot shower, I scrubbed my arms to get rid of the stickiness and rinse off the smell of hot grease and pancakes. But as I climbed into bed, something was nagging at me, that feeling that I've forgotten something important. I was pricked with uneasiness, then pushed it away to let go of the day.

Two days later, Arlene called. When I heard her voice on the phone, it rushed back to me—the deaths, their anguish, the funerals. Arlene was hesitant, even apologetic. But they needed to know, could I do the funerals? I stammered out apologies, then stopped myself. There was no excuse for it. I had failed them, fled from this darkness. Now it was time to go into it with them. When I called, Janey brushed away my apologies and thanked me wearily. I offered to come to their house, but she told me Jim wasn't up to talking to anybody. Another brother, a retired cop, had gone up to the house in New York to take care of things there. The family would meet with me at the funeral home.

I tried to piece together what happened from news reports. Kevin had strangled Beth first, using only his hands. Later, when Jenny got home from school, he strangled her with a belt or some kind of ligature. He put them both in their beds, tucked the sheets around their bodies. The next day, he shoveled the driveway, then went back into the house, sat on the steps leading upstairs to the bedrooms, and drove a steak knife into his femoral artery. The bodies lay there two more days. His mother had called and called. When no one answered the phone, she asked the police to check the house.

Reporters questioned a neighbor, a coworker, a family member. His job was too stressful, his boss too pressuring. He was being treated by a psychiatrist who did too little, or the wrong thing. He was depressed, anxious about his job and his marriage. For a time, the family had been active in a religious group some considered a cult; maybe that was the explanation. If only he had gotten help. If only she had left him, and taken her daughter with her. If only she had reached out to someone. If only we had known.

If only. That cry of protest, howled against what can't be undone. Useless, hurled into the black hole of "why?"

On Sunday morning I told the congregation what had happened. From their shocked faces, I realized most of them were hearing it for the first time. I was surprised the news hadn't gotten around already. Janey and Jim had lived in a row house (her grandparents') around the corner for years. Not too long ago they had moved away to an inner-ring suburb, a short drive from the city, but distant by local reckoning. So no one would have just run into them in the park or the grocery store. And it seemed they had been holding these horrors close. I kept the story spare and announced the arrangements. Viewing and visiting today and tomorrow, funerals at the funeral home on Tuesday.

It started snowing after lunch, big wet flakes dropping a slushy layer on the streets. When Gary and I drove to the viewing, the roads were mostly clear, but on the side street next to the funeral home, the tires slipped and then we slid sideways. I got out and inched my way along the sidewalk.

Usually the Saints used McCully's, the funeral home a block from the church that was owned by a longtime member. I hadn't been to this one before. I introduced myself to the funeral director, who ushered me into the dim room where about twenty people were gathered. Jim was standing next to his sister's coffin, his face stunned and vacant. I put a hand on his shoulder, murmured condolences. Beth had been in her early forties but looked younger, her face unlined except around her eyes. At fourteen, Jenny looked childish still, dressed in a pink sweatshirt with a little locket resting on her chest, her long light brown hair fanned out over her shoulders.

Visiting hours began at three, and ordinarily that would mean a rush of new arrivals. Not today. Gary came in alone and went over to Janey. I moved around the room introducing myself; almost everybody there, it seemed, was a relative of Jim. Most of them had not seen Beth and her family since they had moved away, separated by distance and alien choices. People in this community stayed in place, most of them; they didn't have the kind of jobs you move for. Maybe they didn't go to church as their parents had, but they didn't go off and join some church nobody ever heard of, either. So maybe Beth had already seemed lost to them, even if this gruesome ending was nothing anyone had expected.

I wondered how these stricken people were making sense of what no one can explain. No one had said anything about how these two died, maybe for the obvious reason. What was there to say? But it was my job to say *something* as I spoke over these two bodies tomorrow. And more and more, as I lived among these formidably taciturn people as their pastor, I thought it was my job to say what they left unsaid, to speak of the unspeakable. I started to probe a little at the edges of this raw wound. "So young, both of them, and dying like this." People nodded mutely or shook their heads, brushing away tears. No one mentioned the killings, or the killer's name. I was struck by the silence, and their faces: stunned, sad, bewildered, but no signs of anger. Janey said simply, "This wasn't like him. He must have been out of his mind."

I joined a little group of men. One looked about forty, broad shouldered; though the room was hot, he wore a Ravens jacket snapped closed. Another was older, a worn-looking, light-blue blazer hanging off his thin frame. Another, Beth's brother Don, the retired cop, was slumped forward in an armchair, his large veined hands on his knees. I sank to my knees, holding on to the arm of his chair. "Oh my God, what a terrible shock. Janey told me you went to the house."

He raised his head to take my hand. "Thanks for coming, Pastor."

"Not a place you ever imagined you would go. How are you doing?"

He shook his head. "It was bad."

I stood up and turned to the others. "You hear about this kind of thing on the news, but who knew it would ever happen to anyone you know?"

The guy in the Ravens jacket sighed. "I guess it was their time."

The man next to him nodded. "Everything happens for a reason."

I let my face go stony. The man in the Ravens jacket started to shift uneasily from one foot to another, and then said, "I don't know; maybe he was depressed or something. Why would somebody go off like that?"

The silence grew, as we contemplated that unanswerable question.

Then Don got up abruptly and said, "What's the difference? It's done."

I signaled Gary it was time to go. Outside, I took a deep breath of cool air, relieved to be out of the stifling heat. The wet snow had stopped, and the slush on the street was melting. Back at the parsonage, I shed my clergy garb and pulled on an old sweater and my favorite cords, worn to velvety softness. We put together a makeshift supper, and then I trudged through the hall into the dark church. My study was damp and chilly. I debated turning on the heat but then decided to tough it out. The utility bills were killing us.

I read over the funeral service. I was counting on the words to sustain me as I stood next to those two coffins tomorrow. The language is formal, drawing on words and images from Scripture to give voice to lament and thanksgiving. Gratitude for the life we have shared with the one who has died. Grief for what has been lost. Proclamation of the church's resurrection hope, the promise that death is not the end. In the sermon, I would acknowledge the violence of these deaths, and the shock waves that slammed us in deaths like these. It was my job as well to say something about where God is, even—maybe especially—in these godforsaken deaths. I would not, could not, even try to explain what had happened, but I felt compelled to counter, somehow, that credo that "everything happens for a reason." I don't believe—can't believe, won't believe—that God causes suffering.

Still, there's no doubt that God allows suffering. For me, some glimmer of what this might mean is revealed on the cross, where God refused to save God's own Son, and suffered through and with him; on the cross, where Jesus refuses to answer violence with violence. This God feels true to me: a God who suffers for us and with us; a God who doesn't save us from harm and danger, but meets us in it. Yet I had to admit that in my own darkest moments, I have wished for some other God than this vulnerable one; a God who will act decisively to save me and those I love, not this awful, helpless, hand-wringing God.

Everything happens for a reason. I'm repelled by that stark credo and its stoic acceptance of all the terror of this world. But I have come to understand why some might affirm it. If everything happens for a reason, at least Somebody has a plan, and if God's ways are inscrutable to us, well, so be it. If every event has its place in some larger design, then our suffering has meaning and gravitas. If everything happens for a reason, we have an airtight defense against doubt and regret, a heart sealed against the corrosion of "if only" and "what if" and "why."

I remembered William Sloane Coffin's sermon at the funeral of his twenty-four-year-old son, killed in a car accident, and pulled it up on my screen. It is a vehement "No!" to those who tried to comfort him with platitudes about God's will: "The one thing that should never be said when someone dies is, 'It is the will of God.' Never do we know enough to say that. My own consolation lies in knowing that it was not the will of God that Alex die; that when the waves closed over the sinking car, God's heart was the first of all our hearts to break." Those words seemed like gospel truth to me; I would use them tomorrow, and not for the last time.

For the Gospel reading, I decided to use the raising of Lazarus, a story that begins with heartfelt reproach to an absent God. Jesus gets an urgent summons from his friends Mary and Martha. Their brother Lazarus is ill. Jesus delays, and by the time he gets there, Lazarus has been dead for four days. Martha goes out to meet Jesus and says, "Lord, if you had been here, my brother would not have died." Mary greets him with the same words: "Lord, if you had been here, my brother would not have died." The story ends with Jesus calling Lazarus out of the tomb, a spectacular resurrection. But I would end the reading in the middle of the story, as mourners weep at the tomb.

In the sermon I repeated Martha and Mary's reproach, "If you had been here, Lord, our brother would not have died," and then turned it into a question: "Where were you, Lord, when my sister and my niece died? Where were you, Lord, when my aunt and cousin died? Where were you, Lord, when death came so abruptly and violently to this mother and daughter?" Against my own resistance—for who can dare to answer this question?—I answered it by saying, "God does not save us from our own violence. But when death came for Beth and then for Jenny; when Kevin took life into his own hands, and took their lives; when Kevin took justice into his own hands, and took his own life— God *was* there. God saw it all, just as he had seen his own Son murdered. God saw it all, and wept. God saw it all, and God's own heart was the first to break."

The next day was warmer, a pale sun behind the clouds. At the funeral home I went to stand with the little group in front of the coffins. My stomach flipped. Was that a faint shadow of bruising around Beth's neck, showing through the heavy makeup? I turned away and scanned the small crowd, maybe forty or forty-five people. Except for Gary, no one from the congregation was there. It was a weekday morning; maybe they had come last night.

The funeral director caught my eye; when I nodded, he started the canned music, a sung version of the Lord's Prayer accompanied by what sounded like a hockey rink organ. I stepped to the lectern as the vocalist wailed to the crescendo, "For-ever and EVER, Aaaaaaaamen." I felt buzzed with nerves yet oddly removed, observing myself from a few feet away. As always, once I began, I felt held up by the familiar cadences of the funeral service.

At the end, I walked over to the coffins and placed my hand on each in turn for the commendation. In a few more years, I would know these words by heart: "Into your hands, O merciful Savior, we commend your servant Beth. Acknowledge, we humbly beseech you, a sheep of your own fold, a lamb of your own flock, a sinner of your own redeeming. Receive her into the arms of your mercy, into the blessed rest of everlasting peace, and into the glorious company of all the saints in light." And then again, over Jenny's body. The funeral director took it from there, instructing the mourners to "pay their last respects." As people filed past the coffins, they were subdued, even grim—or maybe just drained.

I watched as the coffins were loaded into two hearses and then took the shotgun seat of the lead hearse. On the way to the cemetery, I asked the funeral director about the visitation the night before; were there more neighbors and friends, some members of Saints and Sinners?

"No, not really. Just the family, pretty much." When I went silent, he added, "Pastor, you'll find with something like this, people don't come around, mostly."

The hearses pulled up next to the awning set up a few yards away from the grave, concealed under a mat of crinkly fake grass. I imagined the deep hole underneath. The two coffins would be buried one on top of the other. The pallbearers lined up on either side of each hearse and took hold of the casket handles. I stepped in front of them to lead the procession to the grave. The grass was soaked from yesterday's snow, and the ground squished under my shoes.

When we reached the grave, I stood between the two coffins and watched the mourners straggle over the matted grass. The closest relatives and older people sat on the folding chairs set in two short rows under the awning. Others stood behind them in a wide semicircle. I scanned the small crowd to find Gary. He was standing near the back, his face somber and composed. He looked back at me, and I felt steadied, deeply glad he was there. A light breeze stirred my hair. I blinked back tears and read the short service. I poured sand on Beth's coffin: "We commit her body to the ground, earth to earth, ashes to ashes, dust to dust." And again, for Jenny.

The graveside service ends with the pastor blessing the people. I paused for a minute, squinting in the sun; their figures were silhouetted against a light-blue sky streaked with clouds. I lifted my arm as I said the benediction, turning slowly to look from one face to the next. Then the funeral director stepped up and directed people to go to their cars. I walked over to Janey and Jim, folding them in wordless embraces.

As the little crowd dispersed, a man in a gray overcoat lingered behind and then came up to me. "Thanks, Pastor. This was a tough one for you, I'm sure."

"Yep." I shook his outstretched hand. "An awful thing. I'm so sorry for all the family."

Our hands unclasped, and I waited for him to turn away. I could see the funeral director out of the corner of my eye, shifting from one foot to the other. The cemetery workers were waiting a few yards off, ready to get on with the burials. Gary was standing at a discreet distance, waiting for me.

The man stood looking at me for a long moment, his face unreadable. Then he said, almost fiercely, "You were born for this." He walked off, his overcoat flapping around his legs.

I felt anointed by his words. Blessed. Unequipped, but held up and lit by grace.

A few days went by. I felt troubled and unsettled by the Saints' absence. Why hadn't they come? I hoped some of them were showing up now for Janey and Jim. Arlene, surely, and maybe she and others were bringing food, coming to visit, sending cards. One morning, I stopped to talk with Betty, setting up for Sunday in the sacristy, and asked hesitantly if she and Harry had been able to get to the viewing. She said, "We didn't really know them. They weren't from here." I bit back my protest. What about Janey? And what did it matter, whether or not anyone knew Beth? She was Jim's sister! But she had moved away years ago. *Not from here.*

Marda called to ask how the funerals had gone. We'd become friends at seminary, holding each other up. She'd been ordained a year before me and had landed in a church about an hour from

Saints and Sinners; when I'd gotten my call, we'd rejoiced to be close again. When I told her none of the Saints had come, she was indignant. My voice cracking, I reminded her that I too had let Janey down, even forgotten all about these terrible deaths for a couple of days. I told her what Betty had said. Maybe others felt the same, disconnected from someone who'd moved so far away and taken up a life so different from theirs. Marda protested, "What about you? They should have been there for their *pastor*."

Still ruminating, I mused about it with Gary. He was blunt. "They're tribal."

That seemed too stark, though I felt a minatory chill as I considered it. If it were true, how would the Saints ever be able to welcome newcomers who were not like themselves? If it were true, how would the Saints overcome their own divisions, the unspoken rivalry between families, the silent standoffs?

If it were true, how would the Saints ever accept me as one of their own?

# CHAPTER 10

## ENTERTAINING ANGELS

I leapt to my feet when the door buzzer rasped and ran to the office door; through the small, square window I saw a very tall African American man, his long face framed by a beard and Afro threaded with gray. I hesitated. Opening the door to a stranger was a risk, one that I probably shouldn't have taken as often as I did. But his expression seemed mild behind wire-rimmed glasses; so I unlocked the door, pulled it open, and invited him in. Stooping a little, he shook my hand and handed me his card: *Vernon Jones*. I saw he was the president (and entire membership, as it turned out) of All That Jazz, a group he'd started to promote jazz performances and musicians. Always on the lookout for venues and partners, he'd been cruising around the neighborhood and noticed the banner over the door, "Wayside Stage." So he'd stopped to find out if we had a performance space and an interest in hosting an event.

I felt a surge of triumph. That banner was the subject of simmering resentment. Some in the congregation had been furious when it first went up over the office door, complaining that no one would know we were a church. But council had approved the banner, and I'd coolly reminded them of that. Of course their real grievance was that this community-theatre group had breached our building in the first place. Having lost that battle, they lost no opportunity to raise objections to whatever the troupers proposed.

Wayside Stage had arrived at Saints and Sinners in much the same way as Vernon, knocking at the door to ask if we had a stage. Their group was twice the size of All That Jazz, comprising two people instead of one: Michael, a playwright, composer, and devotee of musical theater, and Ruth, his wife, an actor, singer, and costume designer. Michael was a small, compact man with a shock of white hair and an intense, slightly impatient air. Ruth had a warm voice with a touch of a southern accent, a wide smile, large brown eyes, and a mild expression; she was a couple of inches taller and a dozen years younger than Michael. They lived a few blocks away in a row house that had belonged to Ruth's parents, and they dreamed of creating a true community theater, with an audience drawn from the neighborhood.

I'd brought them downstairs and pulled back the heavy dark-red curtain to unveil our stage. That sent up a cloud of dust as the curtain jerked open, bunching up in a few places where the hooks had come off the rod. Behind the bedraggled Christmas trees and assorted detritus from Winter Wonderland, the back wall was painted a muddy green, with a white rectangle on one side; someone had painted around a storage cabinet, it seemed. I felt embarrassed by the clutter and struggled to stifle a string of nervous apologies.

Then I saw Michael looking around appraisingly as Ruth's face lit with excitement. "This is perfect!" she enthused. "Well, we'd need to fix the curtain, and add more lighting," Michael said, "and we need storage space for props and stage sets." I groaned inwardly; just what we needed, more stuff in the basement. And it wouldn't be easy to explain to the Saints why I thought it would be a good idea to make space for a theater company's equipment, after all the assaults I'd mounted against the Saints' own stuff.

As I'd expected, this had been a hard sell. The whole point, as they saw it, was getting more people in church, and they'd been bemused or openly skeptical about how musical theater might advance that end. In response, I exhorted them to consider hospitality as our mission, including sharing our space with neighborhood groups.

"What will we get out of this, Pastor?" one of the Saints had asked when I raised the possibility of housing the community theater.

"They'll help us become who we're meant to be!" I shot back. When he looked blank, I prompted, "You know, welcoming the stranger as if he were Christ. And remember that story about Abraham feeding those guys who turned out to be messengers from God? 'Entertaining angels unawares'!" He'd shrugged and replied doubtfully, "If you say so, Pastor."

I took this as a promising start. I figured Constance would view the theater askance, but I also knew she was unlikely to oppose it directly. And this time I thought I'd have council in my corner, since the last elections had taken a startling turn. Ordinarily, council membership was distributed by a tacit apportionment. I'd discovered this on the first round of elections, when Chuck, then council president, had surprised me by making sure there was a Feldman on the election slate. As a son of Constance and George, he dutifully represented their views on most matters; at the same time, he was an important crossover figure, since in a rare show of independence, he attended the late service (Feldman territory by tacit and longstanding consensus). The Feldmans generally eschewed official positions on council or as committee heads, instead exercising their influence in other ways. Still, they did regularly find one among their ranks to fill "their" council seat. The Ausdauers' smaller numbers precluded their maintaining an official family member on council, but Constance wielded her power from the sidelines as financial secretary, and council always included a representative from the early service who was effectively her proxy.

This year's elections, though, had yielded a council with no representatives from either family. I wasn't sure what to make of it. Had both houses declared a plague on me? Would any council decree be doomed to die of neglect, without the official endorsement of the matriarchs' representatives? Maybe it was an opportunity, an opening to break out of the stalemate that resulted from the Saints' commitment to peace at any price. This could be my chance to shake things up, and I resolved to make the most of it.

I'd started by relocating meetings from the stuffy council room to the dining room of the manse. We met once a month on a weeknight; about half the council members came directly from work, so I started setting out snacks and then decided to offer a simple supper. They'd received the spread with surprised smiles, and eating together around the big table created a new ease in our meetings. I had come to dread council meetings with their deadly slog through turgid agendas. Now our meetings were lit up with new energy; we laughed and talked, interrupting one another in our eagerness to get ideas out on the table and make things happen.

When I brought up the possibility of hosting Wayside Stage, most of them were excited about a partnership that might give us new visibility in the neighborhood. I warned that this was going to involve more than the hospitality we extended to other groups using our space—the parents-and-toddlers groups who met on weekday mornings, or the yoga classes held a couple of evenings a week. Even those had created some friction. The yoga instructor groused that the moms didn't vacuum the carpet properly; and the Sunday school teachers complained that the yoga instructor didn't put the kids' tables back where they belonged.

The community theater would be using the building a lot more intensively. We'd have to coordinate with them as they scheduled auditions, rehearsals, and performances, and make space for their stuff. That meant getting those Christmas trees off the stage, and finding someplace in the basement to store the props and costumes for their biggest production: Dickens's *A Christmas Carol*, set to music composed by Michael. And yes, that would happen around the same time as Winter Wonderland. Martha looked uncharacteristically somber at the prospect of mounting Winter Wonderland with new logistics to manage, but rallied quickly. Then there was the storage question. Charlene's face fell at the prospect of rearranging the basement yet again. I couldn't imagine how she'd find room for the trees while also making space for *A Christmas Carol*. But then she said, "Pastor, I'll figure it out. Let's do it!"

We'd weathered the first round of *A Christmas Carol*, opening right after Winter Wonderland. There'd been tense moments on both sides. Some of the Saints were heard to mutter that this was our church. Why did we have to climb over racks of costumes and keep the stage clear until the last minute so they could rehearse? I'd had a difficult exchange with Michael as *A Christmas Carol* came down to the wire; he insisted the dress rehearsal had to happen right after Winter Wonderland closed. We'd never taken it down that fast before, and I felt guilty for lashing the exhausted Saints into action before they'd had even a day to recover. But we'd survived the first season. Winter Wonderland always inspired the Saints to heroic efforts, and our spirits were lifted by the crowds who came to enjoy the food, lights, and trees. After that ended, the fellowship hall usually took on a dispirited air, with the Saints rattling around amid drooping decorations and half-dismantled sales tables. This year, the hall hummed with activity as performances of *A Christmas Carol* drew enthusiastic audiences, many of them people who hadn't come to our events before.

So Wayside Stage was now officially lodged at Saints and Sinners, and their banner over our door had just the effect I had hoped for, signaling our interest in neighborhood ventures. Now it had delivered Vernon to our door; or maybe he'd been blown in by the Holy Spirit, that wind of new life. Vernon wasn't a musician himself, he told me, but he loved jazz and had made its preservation a kind of personal crusade. He especially wanted to find neighborhood venues like ours, churches or community centers that could accommodate jazz performances and draw audiences.

As I took him downstairs to see our stage and fellowship hall, I felt gratified to notice the upgrades we'd made. Charlene had undertaken a redo of the hall, giving the dingy beige paint a fresh coat of creamy white, with an accent wall in apple green. When we'd taken down the valances that covered the windows, we'd found that the fabric was not only dusty but succumbing to dry rot. I'd hesitated; it was decent fabric, upholstery grade, but I couldn't imagine it would survive laundering. So I snuck it into Georgia's trash bins. Jill and Cheryl had taken charge of the bulletin boards, replacing faded construction paper and old photos with colorful

borders and more recent pictures (the Feldmans featured promi-
nently in most of them, I couldn't help but notice; still, the update
projected a positive image of us as a lively multigenerational congregation, and no one besides the Saints had to know that all these
people came from one family).

Michael and Ruth had tackled the stage. Ruth examined the
bedraggled curtain but decided it was beyond repair, even with her
considerable skills as a seamstress. We'd taken it down and consigned it to the trash one weekend when George and Constance
were away. Michael had painted the back wall black, inciting fierce
protests from some members; they hadn't been mollified when I
explained this was the standard backdrop for a working stage. Our
antique sound system didn't work, but Michael had put together an
impressive array of speakers, amps, microphones, and receiver, and
I thought he would probably loan it to the jazz concert.

Vernon turned in a slow circle to take it all in and then breathed,
"This is perfect." That was all it took to set me off; I could almost
feel the electricity zapping across my synapses as my mind raced
with possibilities. He had the musicians, we had the venue. I imagined jazz musicians filling the place with sound as appreciative lis-
teners applauded the riffs. Still, I reminded myself firmly not to get
carried away; I couldn't promise Vernon anything without getting
Wayside Stage and the Saints on board. Michael and Ruth were
likely to jump on it. They wanted to make Wayside Stage into a
community arts center, a venue for other performances. I wasn't so
sure I could deliver the Saints. The Feldmans were justly proud of
their relatives in the choir, prodigiously talented singers, but I had
no reason to think they'd support a musical event that didn't feature
their members. Most of the Saints hadn't raised any objections to
Wayside Stage, but it had turned out—not for the first time—that
this didn't mean they endorsed the idea, or that they were prepared
to do more than abide it. Council had been enthusiastic at first, but
even they had become notably reserved as others grumbled about
the inconveniences of accommodating the troupers.

Vernon was hoping to plan a jazz concert for this summer.
That was traditionally a slack time for congregational activities,
so the concert wouldn't be bumping up against other programs.

An evening of music — maybe the Saints would even welcome that diversion in the city's long hot summer.

Maybe. But this time, I vowed to approach the project with zeal tempered by a steely realism. Since Vernon would be hiring the musicians, it didn't seem as if this would cost us any money beyond the negligible expense of lighting the hall and powering the amps. The event would cost time and energy, though, and chances were I'd be paying heavily in those currencies. Maybe most of all would be the price exacted by the Saints' resentment or reluctance. Some of them were ferociously opposed to Wayside Stage and would hate this on principle, once they knew Michael and Ruth were in on it. But I wasn't going to be deterred by the risk of conflict. That would be succumbing to the Saints' own reflexive avoidance of taking any action that might disturb anyone.

Besides, we all agreed (loosely speaking) that the congregation needed to reach out to new neighbors. Admittedly, what most of them had in mind was attracting people who would show up on Sunday mornings and then join our ranks, improving our weekly offering and providing a fresh source of volunteers. Our flagging energy and ever-more-dire balance sheets had given me a certain renegade sympathy for this point of view, but I continued to oppose it publicly. If we had no clear purpose beyond staying open, what was the point? Besides, who would want to join us just to help warm the seats, do the work, and pay the bills? We should welcome and serve people around us because that's what Christians were supposed to do, I admonished the Saints.

But even the few who had supported projects like Wayside Stage had done it with the ultimate goal of increasing our membership. They were willing to try unorthodox methods to raise our visibility in the neighborhood — desperate times require desperate measures — but they too expected a payoff, eventually, in congregational growth. When I'd first arrived at Saints and Sinners, I was confident we could have it both ways. Generous hospitality and openness to the community would draw people to us, and the rest would follow: new energy, more members, a renewed sense of purpose. After several years, I'd become more reserved in making that claim. Hospitality to the neighborhood was a ministry, not a transaction calculated to build our membership rolls. The newcomers around us needed what we had to offer. Though they might appear advantaged by their youth, education, and affluence, they too were lonely, uncertain, and vulnerable, in need of wholeness and healing, just like us.

The Saints were not convinced, and that was putting a positive spin on it. A few dismissed it angrily; if people recognized their need for God, let them come find God where we did, in Sunday worship. Most were bemused, if not outright baffled, at the notion that these privileged neighbors were our mission field. Some of the Saints felt neglected and disdained by people they regarded as interlopers. In truth, some of the newcomers did treat longtime blue-collar residents with snobbish condescension, when they considered them at all. Most of the Saints resisted my efforts to get them to invite these strangers to church. "Our doors are open," they told me through gritted teeth. They felt rebuffed by the neighbors' indifference to our events and invitations, and unwilling to court further rejection. I felt a bit deflated myself, and I'd only been at it a few years; the Saints had endured two generations of decline. And some of them just didn't want these people around. They viewed the newcomers as rootless, heedless, and spoiled. Besides, most of the Saints simply didn't have the energy or the desire to bother with people who were going to be around for only a few years.

So whom could I count on for a jazz concert? As I'd expected, Michael thought the concert was a perfect fit for Wayside Stage's promotion of community arts. They'd be on hand to run the sound equipment and help manage the audience. But he and Ruth were going away for a month, so they would not be around to publicize the event or sell tickets. When I reported to council about the planned concert, Harry was enthusiastic. He loved jazz, and he and Betty would be there, he assured me. Georgia offered to help with publicity and hospitality; we'd offer refreshments during intermission. Martha shook her head; she and Bob spent most summer weekends at their trailer at the beach, and they wouldn't be available. The others were affable but noncommittal.

The bottom line: this jazz concert would be yet one more event I'd be trying to produce with very little support. More than once

I'd forged ahead anyway with some quixotic notion of inspiring the Saints by example, only to find most of them unmoved. I was worried too that even those who were willing to take risks and try new things were getting worn out. I liked to think of myself as stalwart, resilient, and determined, but in truth I was beginning to lose heart myself. I'd been operating like an inexperienced poker player rendered reckless by a few lucky wins, willfully disregarding my bad bets and mounting losses. Now I had to settle down and pay attention to the odds. The jazz concert looked like a losing hand—time to fold.

So why did I decide to double down instead?

I could say it was Vernon. I'd warmed to him right away, moved by his passion for jazz and his persistent efforts to support musicians. I loved his gentle presence and, as I got to know him, felt touched by his dedication to his aging mother. He understood church too, in a way that few of my friends did.

Then there was my own weakness for doomed projects. I couldn't seem to resist a hopeless cause. That combination of denial, delusion, and sheer perversity sometimes served me well. I'd pulled off a few big wins at Saints and Sinners, against the odds. In the long term, even I could see that it was a losing strategy. But once again, my genius for rationalization kicked in to override my careful accounting.

The real problem, I decided, was that we had entered these partnerships with too little on the table. Time after time, we'd set up agreements with neighbors—the parents-and-toddlers groups, the yoga classes, the Head Start center that shared our building, Wayside Stage—that involved minimal investment on our part. They used our space. In exchange, we got rent from Head Start; from the others, we hoped to trade in the currency of goodwill and heightened visibility. Maybe it was time to try a more active partnership.

Without it, the jazz concert wasn't going to work. Vernon had let me know early on that he needed help to build an audience. For a time, he'd had a place he could use for a series of concerts, and a small grant to help fund them. But he'd lost that space and spent the grant; that had left him driving around the city in search of a new venue. He'd been relieved to find us, and hopeful that he could draw on our neighborhood connections to fill the house.

I did the math. The fellowship hall could accommodate about 125 people. Vernon needed close to a thousand dollars to pay the musicians, and he couldn't go ahead without knowing we had a decent shot at that. We agreed we couldn't charge more than $15 at the door and $10 for a ticket in advance.

Only $1,000. It was so little, by most measures. I thought of meetings I'd attended at affluent suburban congregations faced with an unexpected capital expense: a furnace failure, a roof repair, a parking lot pocked with potholes from a snowy winter. Council would pass a basket for pledges and get commitments of $30,000 or $35,000 on the spot. That was out of the question at our small blue-collar congregation; even at Saints and Sinners, though, $1,000 represented only a sliver of our annual budget. But there was no way I was going to ask the Saints to come up with it. I thought of the hours of work they put in to raise a few hundred dollars at a pancake supper or spaghetti dinner.

So I looked at Vernon and declared, "We'll buy fifty of the tickets."

His face lit up. With a commitment of $500, he could risk the rest. He'd work on selling another fifty and we'd hold twenty-five tickets for people walking in on the night of the concert. We exchanged exuberant high fives and picked a date in late July.

When my adrenalin high wore off, I returned to earth with a sickening thud. What had I done? I had no authority to spend unbudgeted money, so when I'd said, "*We'll* take fifty tickets," that "we" actually meant "*I.*" No doubt I could sell a few of those tickets, but there was also a good chance I'd be stuck with some of them, and then what? I didn't look forward to explaining to Gary that I'd dropped a couple of hundred or more on unused tickets to a jazz concert. I felt a spike of anxiety followed by fierce resolve. One way or other, I was going to unload those tickets.

I set out on my sales campaign. I announced the concert in the *Herald Angel* — I could probably count on Allison, at least. I sent flyers to our usual mailing list of local congregations and ran notices in our local community newspaper. I mobilized my sales force, which ultimately consisted of Georgia. When I confessed what I'd done, she agreed with a grimace to sell ten tickets on the condition that I didn't poach any more of the Saints. (I'd already sold two to Harry and Betty, and another pair to Marie and her partner, Tony.) So that left thirty-six. I took tickets wherever I went—yoga classes, clergy Bible studies, the local library, Wayside Park where I accosted people walking their dogs. A few days before the concert, I bought the last ticket myself; Vernon had sold most of his, too.

Then we were hit by an annihilating heat wave, with highs in the triple digits and humidity to match. The fellowship hall had ceiling fans but the windows didn't open; it would be unbearable once we'd packed in all those warm bodies. I swallowed hard and decided to poll council about moving the event upstairs. The sanctuary was equipped with air conditioners bolted to the walls, and the jazz pianist could use our grand piano instead of a keyboard. But many of the Saints were barely putting up with Wayside Stage as it was; some would be outraged by an intrusion into our worship space. There was no time to convene a meeting, so I took the vote by phone and e-mail. Council members were split. That gave me the tie-breaking vote—a sure recipe for resentment, but so be it.

The day of the concert, Georgia came over to help get the refreshments ready, joined by Pam, a council member and ally in the cause of change. We cut up fruit for sangria and filled several heavy glass pitchers with red wine, Cointreau, and fruit juice. Gary arrived in the late afternoon and helped set out cheese and crackers, little sandwiches, bread and dips, and cookies.

A few minutes before starting time, people began to come in and find seats in the pews. As Michael stood up to greet the audience, I looked around at the half-full church and felt a little disappointed; we'd sold more advance tickets than this, along with a few sales at the door. But anyway, we'd made enough money to pay the musicians. If the paid customers didn't show up for the music, that was their loss.

I forgot my disappointment as the church filled with sound. The musicians wove lilting melodies and then broke off into intricate riffs. I couldn't take my eyes off the pianist as his hands raced up and down the keyboard, fingers dancing so fast they were almost a blur. A few more people began to trickle in, and then suddenly there were fifteen or more at the door. Soon the church was as full as it was on Christmas Eve. The audience applauded warmly, and the musicians responded with more elaborate riffs. I looked around the crowd. Harry and Betty were there, along with a few others from the congregation; I recognized some others from the neighborhood, along with many unfamiliar faces. The crowd was more diverse than we'd ever seen on Sunday—lots of young people, many African Americans, a few gay couples.

Right before intermission Georgia, Pam, Gary, and I slipped out to get ready to serve refreshments; Michael would direct the crowd through the hall and into the manse. Almost immediately a bottleneck developed as the hall filled with the slow-moving crowd. We poured sangria into plastic cups and handed out paper cups of seltzer and lemonade. People surrounded the table to fill paper plates with food. Across the room, Michael was signaling me to get the crowd back for the rest of the concert. I herded people toward the door, marveling at their good humor as they squeezed back into the hall again and up the stairs to the church.

At the end of the second set, the crowd broke into wild applause and cheers, clapping and stamping their feet until the smiling musicians obliged with an encore, and then another. Finally they set down their instruments and the audience got up to file out into the night. Back at the manse, Gary, Georgia, and I sat down with glasses of lemonade and toasted one another. Georgia sighed with satisfaction and declared, "Sitting in there tonight—I looked around thinking, this is my dream for Saints and Sinners. I would love, love to have it like this every Sunday, the church filled with all kinds of people."

It never happened again. We hosted a few more evenings of jazz, downstairs in the fellowship hall. I'd told Vernon and Michael that I couldn't take the lead on ticket sales again, and we never again had the exuberant crowd we'd drawn that first night. The audiences were small and then smaller, until we reluctantly decided we couldn't do any more. When I wondered why, Michael shrugged and said it was hard to hold people's interest; maybe the novelty had attracted them to the first event, along with my sales push. But jazz devotees had become a niche audience, and the niche was small. (That sounded a lot like church.)

The evening had been an exhilarating success, beyond my wildest dreams. Even so, it hadn't yielded any long-term results, at least not that I could see. It hadn't opened the hearts and minds of the Saints. If anything, it might have aided the campaign against Wayside Stage; as I'd expected, many of the Saints were upset to learn we'd held a jazz concert in the sanctuary. The audience had loved the concert and warmly appreciated our hospitality. But it hadn't paid off in the currency the Saints most cared about; no one who'd come to the jazz concert turned up for our worship services. I'd loved working with Vernon, and we'd developed a warm relationship, but as the jazz programs fizzled and then died, he went away disappointed.

Still, that night had been magical. As the months went by and we weren't able to replicate it, my memories of it were clouded with disappointment. Later, I saw it through a scrim of nostalgia pierced with regret: yet another moment of shimmering possibility that had proved as insubstantial as a dream. It was only much later when I finally could see that night for what it really was: a little glimpse of the kingdom of God.

# CHAPTER 11

## BATTER MY HEART

"The doctor says there's a good chance it's cancer." Her voice was flat, her face blank with shock. I felt a thud of dread, along with reflexive disbelief. Amy was—what, thirty-two, thirty-three years old? She looked healthy, even after a sleepless night had smudged dark circles under her eyes. She'd been having pain in her arm, getting worse until it was bad enough to bring her to the emergency room this morning. Her parents and I were with her now, squeezed into a small examination room. Amy's father, Mel, looked stunned. Barbara, her mother, cried out, "No, God, that can't be right." She turned to me, "Pastor, she doesn't smoke. Never has!"

I took a deep breath. "Let's pray." Barbara dropped her shredded tissue in her lap and grabbed my hand. Amy slid her chair closer to take my other hand and reached for Mel's hand. I paused for a minute, willing myself to keep my voice steady. Out loud I prayed that they might feel God's presence in the midst of this, find strength for this day, and even peace in the storm. Under my words was the prayer of all our hearts: *Please please please. Let her be OK.*

A nurse came in and gave Amy the order for the biopsy tomorrow. It was nearly three o'clock. I had to get back to church, and it was almost time for Amy to pick up their daughter Grace, not quite two years old. Her husband, Daniel, got off from work at five o'clock; Amy had called him a couple of times, but he had not yet heard the doctor's latest pronouncement. "Let's hang on for now," I said with an assurance I didn't quite feel. "We'll know more soon. If it is cancer, we'll have the rest of our lives to worry about it."

Amy lifted her chin, straightened up, and said fiercely, "If it is cancer, I'm going to kick its ass."

The biopsy delivered a roundhouse punch: Lung cancer, stage 4.

Before Amy started chemo, she wanted to come for prayer and Communion. She hadn't been coming on Sundays, weary from tests and appointments and not up to managing the curious questions and inquiring looks she would face in church. We planned to meet for a small gathering the night before her first treatment. We were deep into Baltimore summer, the heat and haze pressing down relentlessly. I decided to set up the parlor as a makeshift chapel; it would take an hour or more to cool down the sanctuary, and the space would feel empty, maybe even desolate, with just a few of us scattered in the pews. I turned on the window air conditioner in the parlor and waited. More often than not, the first surge of power shut down the aging grid, and the unit huffed in defeat before subsiding into inertia. The malfunction was a mystery; the electrical board had been checked and pronounced sound. Regardless, the air conditioner regularly shorted out, sending me into the hall to reset the circuit and try again. This time, it groaned and rattled, then settled into a labored wheezing.

I tugged the furniture around to form a big circle, wondering yet again who had thought it was a good idea to upholster the couch and wing chairs in a white brocade. I hauled some chairs from the fellowship hall for more seating, and just in case, stacked a few extra in the hall. The glass-topped table that I would use for Communion was cloudy with dust, so I went back to the parsonage to find some Windex and paper towels, along with a bag of tea lights to set around the room. Then to the sacristy, to gather wine, wafers, a pottery plate and chalice, and a stack of little plastic Communion cups. I placed the plate and chalice on a freshly ironed white cloth, and then looked over the simple service I had prepared.

The parlor served as a staging area for special occasions — weddings and baptisms, usually — and tonight it felt layered with memories of other times I'd gathered here with Amy and her family. Three years ago, she and Daniel had been married at Saints and Sinners. I had opened the parlor for the florist a couple of hours before the wedding; we had stacked the long boxes holding corsages and boutonnieres on the couch, the bridesmaids' bouquets on the chairs, and the big square box with Amy's bouquet on the glass-topped table. A few hours later Amy had arrived, a little flushed, smiling shyly and lit up with happiness. Her long dark hair, usually falling loose around her shoulders, was swept into a sophisticated updo. Her strapless gown was cut close around the bodice, then flaring into a wide skirt. Her older sister, matron of honor, kept a watchful eye on the train, scooping it off the floor as Amy came up the stairs and into the parlor. The room filled as her bridesmaids followed her in and unpacked the boxes. I greeted everybody while taking attendance silently.

The wedding had actually started on time, to my huge relief. I had another wedding right after this one, a scheduling fluke that had come up when another couple asked for the same day. What were the chances? Weddings were not a frequent event at Saints and Sinners, and ordinarily, couples planned far ahead to secure the church. I had already started marriage preparation counseling with Amy and Daniel and promised them the day they had requested. But then this other couple turned up. The prospective groom was seldom seen at worship, but he was part of the redoubtable Feldman clan (Marge's son), and he and his bride-to-be had already put money down on their reception. I said I'd try to figure out something, but what?

This was a case for the Fixer, my private nickname for the head pastor at Realms of Glory, the large and affluent church about a mile from Saints and Sinners. John was a savvy and generous colleague, always ready to advise me when asked, and I'd appealed to him more than once when perplexed or stymied by the Saints. If he couldn't solve this one, nobody could. He listened as I explained my dilemma. Would it work to do these weddings back to back? He shook his head firmly. The wedding might not start on time. After the ceremony, the photographer would need to line up the wedding party for pictures. And someone would have to clean up discarded tissues or bulletins that had been left in the pews, or flower petals that had fallen on the carpet. Two weddings on the same afternoon, in the same place? It could not be done.

But what if we moved the second wedding to Realms of Glory? I'd need a reliable driver and two cooperative couples. Then I could wed the first couple, dash out of the door in my vestments, and leap into the getaway car in time to get to Realms of Glory for the next round of nuptials. Gary agreed to serve as driver; he'd be waiting at the curb to spirit me away. I'd feared some kind of standoff over who would get to marry on home turf, but both couples proved flexible and easygoing. The back-to-back nuptials had proceeded without a hitch. I'd ended the day weary but triumphant, with my own wedding war story: two weddings on one day!

The parlor served as backstage for baptisms, and Grace's had taken place a year and a half after the wedding. We gathered in the parlor so I could check that everyone had arrived and offer last-minute instructions; parents could soothe a fussy baby in privacy. For my first couple of baptisms I'd erred on the side of caution and asked people to come an hour early; that increased the probability that adults would get there on time, but it misfired badly when it came to the baptismal candidate and any young children involved in the service, for whom an hour in the parlor was an eternity. The trick was to hit the sweet spot: to begin the service on time, all adults present and accounted for, and the baby freshly diapered, well fed, and content; and any other young children not yet fretful with impatience.

For Grace's baptism, the gears had meshed with rare precision. Fifteen minutes before zero hour, everyone was in place. Amy held Grace while Daniel followed bearing bottles and diaper bag. Amy's younger brother looked uncomfortable in his dress shirt and suit, but he grinned as he reached for Grace; he was anointed as her baptismal sponsor (formerly known as godfather, and still called that by everyone but me). Her sister and her husband were also serving as godparents; they arrived right behind Amy and Daniel with their son, a serious four-year-old, and their baby daughter. Grace regarded me warily. She was a round, healthy child with her mother's large dark eyes, and not one to suffer pastors readily; in our rehearsal the week before, she'd let me hold her only briefly before wriggling in protest and reaching toward Amy for rescue. I gave her what I hoped was a disarming smile.

As we lined up at the font, Barbara and Mel were beaming in the front pew, and a little murmur of anticipation went up from the rest of the Saints. I loved this ritual with its hope and expectation: the joy of a new life among us, a heartwarming occasion for a congregation that saw many more funerals than baptisms. The assisting minister poured water into the font as I said the long, beautiful "flood prayer," rich in biblical language and collective memory of God at work. Water is the powerful sign of God's action: water to destroy and kill; water to cleanse and renew; water, as ordinary as dust, and the elixir that sustains all life on this earth. I picked up the sterling silver baptismal shell on the table; I'd polished it the night before, and it gleamed softly under the lights. I dipped it three times into the font and poured water over Grace's head: "I baptize you in the name of the Father, and of the Son, and of the Holy Spirit." She looked mildly affronted. I blotted the water off her head and signed the cross on her forehead in scented oil.

Then I took Grace into my arms to bring her around the sanctuary. Baptism wasn't supposed to be a baby show, we'd been admonished in seminary. But I loved the ritual of introducing the newly baptized to the congregation, and relished any excuse to get my hands on a baby. I lofted her up so everyone could see her face as I walked down the aisle, explaining as I went that they were looking at the newest member of the body of Christ on earth. Grace's face crumpled and she began to cry. Fair enough, I said to her and the congregation. She didn't know what had just been done for her in baptism, but Christian life was no cakewalk, and a little protest wasn't out of line. When she escalated to howls, I race-walked the last few steps back up the aisle to hand her over to her father.

Tonight, the parlor would serve as our chapel, a place to huddle in hope and fear, and to surround Amy with prayer. It had been my joy to bear witness as Amy and Daniel had exchanged their marriage promises, and to pour the water of baptism on their little girl. I hadn't expected that we would meet in this parlor to bolster Amy for chemo. I felt filled with grief for what they had already lost, and heavyhearted to contemplate what might come. But I felt grateful too, for the solemn gift that was mine, to walk with them as their pastor.

People began to arrive just as I finished lighting the candles. Amy came in with Grace clinging to her, legs wrapped around Amy's waist. Behind them were Amy's parents, her brother, her sister and brother-in-law, followed by five or six others who crowded into the entryway: Barbara's sister Arlene with her daughter, Amy's cousin; a woman I recognized as another of Barbara's sisters; and two others about the same age, probably more sisters. Mel told me there were others on their way, trawling the neighborhood for parking. I did a quick count and pulled a few extra chairs from the office. I hadn't taken account of the cousins and aunts and uncles who might come tonight; Amy's big extended family almost filled the room themselves.

Then there were Daniel's parents, huddled in the back. Three young women arrived together, looking as if they had come straight from work in their "business casual" summer skirts and jackets; I thought I recognized two of them from Amy's wedding, bridesmaids maybe. They looked subdued and scared as they went over to hug Amy and then settled into chairs. As more people came in, I headed downstairs for more chairs. A couple of the men saw me bumping two chairs up the stairs and went down to get more. I dashed through the office into the sacristy for more Communion wafers and another stack of cups.

I had never done a healing service before. I'd turned to *Occasional Services* for an outline, then selected a couple of Bible stories on miraculous healing. I'd had misgivings about that. Miracle stories stir up complicated eddies, and I worried about fueling denial and even superstition. Prayer is not magic, and whatever we did in a healing service, we weren't going to be able to control

God. Yet these miracle stories also boldly named the desperate need and hope that brought us into the parlor tonight. So I used those stories and prayed that Amy would be healed, with my unvoiced inner reservation, "whatever form that might take." And why not?

Like everyone else in this room, I wanted Amy to be cured: not just healed in some metaphysical sense, but *cured*, set free from cancer to reclaim the expansive future of young adulthood. Very likely I was the only one in the room who knew that such a cure would be a certified miracle. Almost no one walks away from stage-4 cancer, deemed "treatable but not curable," in the understated language of oncology. So was I misleading them, encouraging an illusory hope? But then again, I didn't know what was going to happen. The occasional outlier or two did survive even the most dire diagnosis. Maybe Amy would be one of them.

I stood up and began with the lament of Psalm 130: "Out of the depths I cry to you." Next, a litany of healing, with petitions that I had added for Amy specifically: that the chemo would attack the cancer, that she would be able to withstand its side effects, that her doctors would care for her with wisdom and compassion. I went over to her and placed my hands on her head as I prayed. At first it felt awkward, this intimacy of this ancient ritual of laying on of hands. Then as I spread my fingers and gently cupped her head, I was filled with tenderness and a flood of compassion. I heard a few people crying and swallowed hard to quell my own tears.

Then Communion. I bent awkwardly over the low table to lift the wafers and then the chalice, grateful for the bracing of ritual. I made my way around the room, bumping into people's knees to place wafers in outstretched hands, and then tip wine into the small plastic cups. After, I raised my hand for the blessing: "May the body and blood of our Lord Jesus Christ strengthen you and keep you in his grace." At her name, Grace looked up, then started to whine and wriggle in Amy's arms. People began to push back their chairs and make their way out.

I locked up, wiped drops of wine off the glass-topped table and dragged the brocade-covered furniture back in place; the chairs could wait for another day. I'd spilled a few drops of wine but luckily I had missed the upholstery; the drips had disappeared into the intricately patterned red and blue carpet. I was exhausted, sad, filled with foreboding as I thought about Amy and the ordeal of treatment. Still, this was the heart of pastoral work, and I felt the awe and weight of it—and even its piercing joy. I had wanted work that used more of myself, that demanded full engagement of both mind and heart. Now that work was mine.

Unequipped. I had prepared for years, and learned more in my years with the Saints. But I was not equipped for what mattered most. Not equipped to deal with the deep questions. Not equipped to stand with people at the edge of life and death as they raged or grieved. Not equipped for the suffering or betrayals or violence that came without warning to shatter an ordinary life. No one is, and part of the work was learning to do it anyway, to come with empty hands and open heart, and let that be enough. It was all we had.

I'd been warned about that, and not only in my ordination sermon. Accepting our limits: that was the deep lesson of pastoral-care training. Paradoxically, there were techniques for that, for leaning into the helplessness. "Nonanxious presence" we'd learned to call it in the professional canons of pastoral care, not without irony. We were trained to cultivate it, the steadiness to abide with others through pain or suffering or conflict, to be wide open to their emotions without being overwhelmed by our own. We'd studied it in pastoral-care classes, practiced it in role playing with one another, and then undergone the rigorous initiation of clinical pastoral education (CPE).

I'd arrived insecure and apprehensive at the start of CPE, unsure I had anything to offer to people in crisis. I had plenty of practice that summer. Car accidents, knife wounds, invasive tumors, seizure disorders, lung and liver and heart and kidney failure: the hospital held an unrelenting procession of every mischance and misfortune that humans are heir to. After ten weeks, I had learned to think on my feet, pray on demand, and trust that I'd have what I needed when I walked into a room filled with stunned or angry or grieving people. I'd finished CPE with new confidence, even as I also recognized that this exercise in extreme pastoral care would not fully equip me for what I'd face as a pastor. I was unlikely ever to confront this density of suffering again, not unless I ended up in a war zone or pandemic. But I knew congregational ministry would present its own challenge. I'd be facing crisis not with strangers, many of whom I had encountered only once or twice, but with people I had come to know and love.

As Amy started chemo, she was resolute, and resolutely upbeat. She was getting care at a top-ranked oncology center, where the full-press treatment for stage-4 lung cancer included repeated counsel to keep up morale and avoid dwelling on the negative. Amy was taking it to heart; she kept telling me she was determined to "stay positive." I felt moved by her resolve, even as I also felt a little tug of concern. Sooner or later, staying positive wasn't likely to sustain her in the face of this mortal danger. But it was getting her through the initial shock of it, at least. I thought about how the trauma team called out to gravely injured patients even as they cut off clothing, assessed vital signs, started IVs, and hooked up heart monitors: "Jimmy! Jimmy! Listen to me. We're taking care of you. You're going to be fine." Sometimes it was even true. And the words themselves could be a lifeline, something to cling to in the riptides of pain and fear.

It wasn't my job to question the value of positive thinking. It wasn't my job, either, to make Amy understand the gravity of her situation. But it *was* my job to let her know I wasn't afraid to talk about death or to hear her fear or anger. When Amy asked me for some Bible verses to bolster her spirits, I copied a few of the healing stories and then turned to psalms, the stalwart confidence of "God is my rock and my salvation," along with lament, "Out of the depths I cry to you."

After the first round of chemo, Amy was scheduled for a scan to see if the treatment was working. The night before we gathered for another healing service, this time in the sanctuary. As people knelt at the altar rail and whispered their requests for prayer, I laid my hands on one head after another and waited for the words to rise in me. Amy called a few days later, her voice excited, light. The tumors were shrinking; one had even disappeared. On Sunday I announced the good news. Barbara and Mel looked hopeful and deeply relieved, and an excited murmur went up from the people scattered in the pews. At the piano bench, Marie called out, her voice husky with tears, "Praise God!"

"Comfort Now My People." That lovely Advent hymn, echoing Isaiah, was our theme for a special service in December. Held on or near the winter solstice, the longest night of the year, the service offered solace for people weighed down by sadness or loneliness or grief, and a refuge from the insistent cheer of the holiday season. This year, we would make it a healing service too, as Amy finished another round of treatment and waited for another series of scans. The theme of Advent is waiting in darkness; the color of the season is blue, the color of hope and the color of the night sky just before dawn. I loved the meditative hush of Advent, and this year our waiting took on another layer of meaning: waiting in darkness with Amy in the shadow of cancer.

Five o'clock, and it was already full dark. I clipped on Scout's leash and headed across the street to the park. Our beloved Shadow had died two years before, succumbing to bone cancer at age twelve. We'd been dogless for so long that it had begun to seem permanent, until Mike had fallen for a blue-eyed puppy who was one of an orphaned litter. Scout was a formidably energetic pup, black with a white blaze on his chest, a husky's curly tail to go with his blue eyes, and the large pointed ears and vigilance of a shepherd. I hustled him along the park, no time for our usual long walk. Back in the kitchen, he sat at full alert as I put his dish on the counter and filled it with kibble. I fixed him with a stern look and warned, "You leave the Christmas tree alone, do you hear me?" I set the dish down in front of him and then went through the hall into the dark church.

I flipped on lights and trudged upstairs through the choir loft to a cramped storage area where the pew candles were stowed. Up and down four times, to bring down eight of them and set them carefully in the brass brackets on either side of the center aisle. It was stone cold. I turned up the thermostat and the furnace rumbled on. And so it went, the familiar rhythms of preparing for worship: check the oil in the candles, the wick in the candle lighter; lift the chalice from its flannel bag; pour wine from the gallon jug; open a fresh cellophane cylinder of wafers and refill the round silver container. Then I slid into a front pew with a bulletin and read through it slowly, imagining myself moving through the liturgy.

When Marie arrived and settled on the piano bench to arrange her music, I lit the candles, then went into the sacristy to put on my alb and my Advent stole, beautifully wrought of silks in shades of blue, purple, and gold. A friend had designed and sewn it as an ordination gift. The colors shaded from dark to light, with an abstract flame running from bottom to top. In gold thread cursive letters spelled out the verse from the prologue of the Gospel of John: "Light shines in the darkness, and the darkness did not overcome it."

About thirty people came, as many as we had in worship on most Sundays, these days. Amy and her family were there, along with some of our Sunday regulars and others who were not usually in our worship. When it was time for laying on of hands, almost everyone came up to ask for prayers: for Amy and friends and relatives with cancer, for comfort in grieving, for a sister going through a divorce, for the strength to stay clean in recovery from addiction. I set my hands on each head, feeling Mildred's soft gray curls under my fingers, Amy's silky wig, Jason's sculpted 'do, firm with product. Something like a warm current surged through me, going down my arms and fingers. I felt amazed by the power of this ritual, and reflexively skeptical at the same time. I didn't believe in this kind of thing, yet it happened.

Maybe this was our true north, these healing services charged with need and alive with hope. On Sundays the Saints seemed downcast and depleted, singing listlessly and going through the motions, and our Sunday attendance kept slipping. Yet many of the same people came to the healing services, and invited friends and neighbors. In the dim light of evening, the same people who were so reserved on Sundays came up for healing prayer with whispered pleas and unashamed tears. For five years now I'd been trying to find a direction for our ministry, with the Saints straggling along with me. I'd run down one rabbit trail after another, in hot pursuit of transformation: the latest program for spiritual renewal, a new approach to evangelism, leadership training that would equip me to lead the charge into new life. The literature of ecclesial self-help seemed bottomless, and I'd succumbed repeatedly to its promises. The three-minute pastor! Six strategies for stronger stewardship! Ten ways to improve your contemporary worship! Thirty-five building blocks of successful congregations! Forty days of purpose! I'd been frustrated when the Saints were unmoved by my exhortations to embrace the latest; now I felt chagrined that I'd tried to sell them all this snake oil.

My clergy colleagues and I often remarked ironically on the doublethink of our own practices. In compliance with denominational guidelines, we tracked worship attendance, maintained membership rolls, and took account of our shaky finances. We crafted strategic plans, set goals, and devised metrics to evaluate how we were doing. Yet the gospel we were called to proclaim stood in stark contrast to this ministry by management. Luther had staked his life on the bold claim that grace alone could save us. Our works, our will, our decisions: none of that had any effect on where we stood with God. These programs were, at best, Band-Aids; at worst, they were deadly distractions. Salvation by programming led us away from the One who really could raise us from the dead.

Success could not be measured by results, or at least not the results we could see or count. Jesus' own ministry had flamed out in abject failure. He'd had a sensational charismatic rise, one that galvanized his opponents; in short order he'd made enemies of religious authorities, and fatally failed to seek the patronage of the Roman government. The crowds following him had proved fickle. He had assembled a willing if inept leadership team—the disciples—but in his hour of need they had betrayed and abandoned him. The long-awaited Messiah was denounced for heresy and treason, left to die a disgraceful death by public execution.

I had been called to ministry, and I'd given my heart to it. But I'd been distracted by the wrong dream, deluded into thinking I could save the Saints. They already had a Savior, and it wasn't me. I was called to be faithful: to do the work in front of me, to serve the people I'd been called to serve, to love the people I'd been given to love. I had wanted more; now, in the shadow of Amy's illness, I was beginning to realize the precious gift that was already mine. Saints and Sinners might well not survive as a congregation. But in the candlelight of the healing services, I saw that the kingdom of God was already among us, and in us.

# CHAPTER 12

## STOP! IN THE NAME OF LOVE

As fireworks burst over the harbor on New Year's Eve, I resolved
to find some new way forward in 2010. March would mark my
fifth anniversary at Saints and Sinners, and in October the congregation would hit a big birthday, 125 years. But last year had been
like the others, a loop of expectation and disappointment. We'd
gain a little ground—some new members, renewed energy, an
unexpected windfall—only to lose it again as newcomers moved
away, older members died, and unexpected expenses snatched
away our momentary surplus. All our plans, our programs, our
prayers: nothing provided more than a momentary stay against the
inexorable drag of decline.

Like congregations all over the country, we were getting crushed
by what economists call Baumol's curse, the bane of enterprises
where productivity remains fixed as costs increase. A worshiping
community can't produce any efficiencies of labor. It takes about
the same time to write a sermon or visit a sick member or conduct
a funeral now as it did centuries ago. Meanwhile, the creep of infla-
tion means it costs more to do the same work. The unavoidable bottom line: congregations cannot survive without a steady increase
of income, and in many of them, income is stable or falling. Fewer

people are attending church, and those who come aren't giving as their parents and grandparents did. Congregations like Saints and Sinners are canaries in the mine, the small and vulnerable places that are the first to falter as the oxygen gets sucked out.

As our prospects drifted downward, I ruminated about what I had done and what I had left undone, hunted by a sense of failure. I tried to shake it off; that kind of thinking was apostasy. I was a Lutheran pastor, after all, and our theology averred that success was not the measure of our worth. What mattered was faithfulness: staying the course and doing the work we were given. That helped sometimes—except that more and more I imagined myself leaving this call, and then felt assailed with guilt at the thought of leaving the Saints to soldier on as yet another pastor walked away. Then there was pride, my besetting sin. I couldn't stand the thought of giving up, admitting defeat—and that's what it felt like, doctrine be damned.

Most of all, I felt heartbroken. The Saints had made me a pastor, accepted me and abided me and loved me. I'd baptized their babies, catechized their teenagers, witnessed their marriage promises, visited them at home and in the hospital and in the nursing home, buried their beloved dead.

Then in February, two epic blizzards slammed Baltimore, rendering the church inaccessible to all but the most intrepid. We'd survived two boiler failures, innumerable roof repairs, rising oil prices, and dwindling membership; but now it looked like we might be taken down by snow—what insurers deemed an "act of God." The Saints were already disheartened. Would they give up altogether after a few weeks without church? On February 6, the snow fell all day and through the night, burying cars, hydrants, bushes, streets, and sidewalks under a thick blanket of white. Ordinarily, we got only a few inches at a time, a snowfall dispatched by a few swipes of a shovel or even a broom. Faced with almost three feet of the white stuff, most people left their sidewalks unshoveled and their vehicles abandoned under mounds of snow. Scout and

I made our way around the neighborhood along the narrow goat trails trampled in the snow by adventurous pedestrians.

I decided to go ahead with worship on Sunday but warned off anyone who had to drive to church, including Gary and Zoe. There was no place to park. On Sunday morning I perched the sandwich board on top of a pile of snow to let neighbors know we were open. Ten people showed up, stamping the snow off their boots and pulling off hats and mittens. Two of them were visitors, neighbors who had seen our sign and couldn't get to their own churches. I felt warmed by the intimacy and energy of our small assembly; after all, Jesus himself had promised that he would show up wherever "two or three are gathered in my name." The worship felt deep, meaningful, authentic—church at its best, another glimpse of the kingdom of God. Yet I couldn't dispel a little twist of worry; a few more weeks of a paltry offering could sink us.

Then the second blizzard hit. As darkness fell, thick snow was coming down. "Snowmageddon," newscasters were already dubbing it. I watched in wonderment as drifts scaled the brick walls behind the manse and engulfed the back steps. The next morning I looked out to a dreamscape, the neighborhood barely recognizable under the cover of obliterating white. The wind had sculpted the snow into otherworldly dips and peaks, the topography of some alien planet.

As I pulled on boots, jacket, hat, and mittens, Scout was already dancing at the door. I snapped on his leash and plunged after him down the front steps. In the park the snow was thigh deep, higher in the drifts. When we'd crested a small hill, I looked back at Saints and Sinners through a scrim of swirling snow. The facade was lightly frosted, wet snow plastered to the brick; as I watched, it seemed the building was slowly disappearing into the dense whiteout. I stood and looked for a long moment. It was beautiful and eerie—unsettling to see the solid building rendered as insubstantial as air.

That afternoon it finally stopped snowing, and a pale sun came out. At day's end, sunset tinted the snow with rose and threw pale blue shadows over the park. People emerged from their houses with cameras; dogs and kids romped joyfully in the drifts. The sun had melted the snow from the bricks, and the church building returned to its reassuring solidity, the bricks and marble softly glowing in the last light.

But the sight of it dissolving into the snow that morning lingered in my mind's eye. Saints and Sinners had anchored this corner for 125 years, but it too was transitory. One day it would be gone, whether converted to other uses, demolished for the land under it, or simply crumbling brick by brick in the long, slow entropy of all material things. And then there was me. I had been here only five years, a tiny sliver of the congregation's history. I wasn't likely to make it even another five as their pastor. In July I would turn sixty. Already, I had more years behind me than ahead of me in this, my one and only life. Was I using it well?

I knew then that I could not stay with the Saints. I had finally admitted that they were not going to rally behind my vision of change, and I did not have the patience and wisdom to become a chaplain to a dying congregation. And maybe I was wrong about their trajectory downward. I'd done everything I could think of to foster growth and renewal, but maybe someone with more experience or training or ability could succeed where I had not—in which case it would be better for them if I moved on sooner rather than later.

Over the next two weeks the neighborhood slowly dug out from the blizzards. The plows came through and, after them, nimble Bobcats that scooped the piles of plowed snow into trucks to dump into the harbor. Bright sunny days sent rivulets of melted snow into the street. People began to ease their cars out of the drifts, getting out for work or errands and then returning to tense standoffs for parking spaces. After two more Sundays of low attendance, people began to come back to church, and before long we'd rebounded to our usual numbers.

But I had changed. I felt calmer and steadier, more able to let go of my frustration and to love the Saints as they were. I felt renewed appreciation for the conversations with homebound members, the music and singing on Sunday, the hush that often followed a sermon or a prayer. At the same time, I resolved to get council to step up. I might be leaving soon, and I did not want them to be helpless and flummoxed in my wake. Every month I forced them to study the budget spreadsheet with its inexorable bottom line: expenses exceeding income. For the last few years, our annual shortfalls had grown: first $15,000, then $25,000, then $30,000. So far, we had met expenses by drawing down cash reserves provided by the legacies of the faithful departed, but those were rapidly dwindling. Each time, the Saints had responded to the budget review by sinking into a glum silence and then moving on. Finally I confronted them with the stark pronouncement: "We've got to grow, merge [with another congregation], or close." I'd never put it to them so baldly, fearful that they would panic or lose heart.

This just went to show that I still didn't know the Saints, because what they did, of course, was ignore me.

Instead, they decided we needed a fundraising committee.

Dominated by the Feldmans, the committee decided to hold a fund-raiser every month. We never netted anything like big money on these; as a response to our current financial meltdown, it was outright delusional. Even the storied Winter Wonderland had never cleared $4,000, and we could be looking at a shortfall of $50,000 by the end of this year. Anyway, who was going to provide the planning and muscle for these events? But I had vowed to make them take responsibility for their own future, and to get behind anything that might motivate them to action.

Thus it was that I found myself singing karaoke.

In the photo, I'm gripping the mike in one hand, the other arm flung out with palm in the gesture of a traffic cop—"Stop!" My black-and-white skirt swirls around my legs; over my red T-shirt, my face is shiny with sweat, flushed with heat, and lit up with an exuberant smile. It was probably the closest I would ever get to my secret ambition to sing in a girl group. And who knew that the Saints would be the ones to take me there?

I admit it: when I first heard the idea, I was skeptical. Spaghetti dinner with karaoke? We'd already held any number of spaghetti dinners that barely cleared expenses. Each time, the congregation was downcast to discover anew that these events were not a draw. It seemed their appeal had palled even for our regulars, and the neighborhood's Gen Xers stayed away in droves. On top of that, the event was scheduled for late June, and we might well end up with a sultry early summer night. Who would want to eat spaghetti under a thick blanket of hot, muggy air? I had to wonder too if karaoke would be the value added that would save this event from what seemed like certain failure. But maybe I was just succumbing to the default pessimism of the Saints. I encouraged the fund-raising committee to invite the troupers from Wayside Stage and to advertise beyond our usual venues.

The week before the event, I saw notices up in the usual places that the Saints frequented: Erline's beauty shop, Schmitt's restaurant (a popular neighborhood place where Marge was a waitress), the corner hardware store. Nothing in the fern bars, though, or the designer coffee shop. They also hadn't gotten the notice into the neighborhood paper, which ran free listings of community events, or e-mailed the president of the neighborhood association that met monthly in the fellowship hall. And when I asked Michael if he and Ruth were coming, he told me the fund-raising committee had never contacted him, so they had decided to go away for the weekend. Fine, I told myself vengefully. The hall would be half empty, and they would have no one to blame but themselves.

By six o'clock it was still 85 degrees and humid, the wet air barely stirring. Downstairs, the fellowship hall was pulsing with sound and the tables were set with red checked plastic cloths, candles in jars, Parmesan cheese in cardboard cylinders, and salt and pepper shakers. Getting closer, I saw that most of them also had little cardboard signs on them: RESERVED FOR ___ (name of family). I felt a flash of exasperation. Once again, the Death to Fellowship Hall was living up to its name. I found a table without a sign, staking out territory for the outcasts.

People started coming into the hall, the usual suspects, traveling in packs. I had pictured date night, something like a bar crowd (minus the alcohol), but it seemed that karaoke was a family affair for the Saints. Our singers from the choir were here in force, of course, and they'd brought their kids and grandkids too. Three of our four teenagers were in the crowd, and Bobby had even come with a date, a petite girl with pale blonde hair pulled into a ponytail. Others were part of the wider circle of the Saints, people who turned up for our events and for baptisms and funerals. I was alone at the outcast table until Renee showed up, wearing a shiny emerald-green top with a deep V-neck and accompanied by two little girls who were visiting her for the weekend.

The karaoke machine was set up in the front, with Janey's son Joey as the DJ. He ran this gig at local bars and community halls most weekends, making extra money. Tonight he was donating his time, and he had brought along his girlfriend, Cindy, and their kids; I had baptized the youngest. As we tucked into plates of steaming spaghetti and sauce, I noticed there was some kind of sign-up going around, as people passed around thick playbooks. Joey cranked up the music, reached into a coffee can on the table, pulled out a slip of paper, and called, "Cindy, lead off!" The crowd gave her a spattering of applause.

She got up and put the headphones on, pulled her shoulders back, and stood with her head down, waiting for the music to cue up. Then she brought the mike close to her mouth and began to sing in a smooth contralto, a classic country song of a woman wronged but defiant. I was caught up by her passion; this performance was personal, a song that was somehow her story. And she couldn't be performing it for the first time tonight, not with this kind of polish and panache. Finishing with a flourish, she pulled off the headset and lifted her long hair off her neck, smiling as the crowd applauded and whistled.

Out of work, out of luck, in and out of love. One after another, the Saints poured their hearts out in these ballads of love and longing. I was exasperated at a fund-raiser that was in effect a kind of closed invitation, but as I listened I understood why they wouldn't easily welcome strangers here. The raw vulnerability in the room reminded me of the healing services: their songs a kind of prayer, karaoke psalms.

I marveled at the talent on display. Janey's exceptional soprano voice carried our choir, but who knew she could yodel? She stepped to the mike dressed in cowboy boots and hat and sang a complicated piece with runs of notes. Eddy and Jacky, uncle and niece from the Feldman clan, offered a clever duet, tossing lines back and forth. Then there was Christian, grandson of Constance and George, a pudgy twelve-year-old with a round face topped with thick black curls. I would have thought he would shun the spotlight, but he strode up to the mike and sang in an assured falsetto. Even the littlest kids, a three-year-old and a four-year old, got up to sing, lisping, "How Much Is That Doggy in the Window?"

Joey called me to get up and sing, and people around me started to chant, "PasTOR, pasTOR," in good-natured teasing. I felt flustered. I loved to sing and had gotten more confident under Marie's tutelage, but I was no match for these supertalented vocalists—not to mention my feeble grasp on popular music. Still, I was forever exhorting the Saints to get out of their comfort zones; so I started flipping through the playbooks. But what I knew seemed either unseemly for a pastor, denigrating to women, or all too revealing. So forget "Will You Still Love Me Tomorrow?," with its one-night-stand vibe, or lyrics that made women look needy or pathetic ("It's My Party and I'll Cry If I Want To") or obsessed with romance ("I Will Follow Him, Wherever He May Go") or serving as sidekicks to bad boys ("Sugar Magnolia"). But what did that leave, except for yet another rendition of "How Much Is That Doggy in the Window?" Then my eyes lit on "Stop! In the Name of Love"—ah, Motown, the favorite dance tunes at my high school.

I put on headphones and picked up the mike. On the monitor in front of me the words bounced in time with the music. I'd forgotten the story line, a classic woman betrayed, pleading for her man, along with the words (except for the chorus). But too late now. As I faltered, the lyrics came faintly through the headphones, and I realized Joey was feeding me a prompt. "Go, Pastor!" Jacky yelled, nodding encouragement. I took a deep breath and belted out the chorus, adding hand motions. The kids laughed and cheered, while others watched me curiously, their smiles affectionate and amused. In mid-wail, I realized that the lyrics were voicing my own lament. I wasn't bemoaning a faithless lover, but day by day my own heart was breaking, all the same, in this ministry that didn't seem to be going anywhere. So tonight this song was my own karaoke psalm: "Stop! In the name of love, before you break my heart."

Even as I'd mercilessly confronted council with the bottom line, I'd encouraged them to plan an anniversary blowout: 125 years! We needed something to boost morale as the shortfall got worse and membership remained stalled, and they could rightly take pride in the fortitude and endurance that had gotten them this far. We formed a celebration committee to plan a festival service followed by a luncheon. Constance unearthed the congregation's incorporation papers, dated late October 1885. This was a double win, since it was close to Reformation Sunday, when Lutherans commemorate Martin Luther's 95 Theses. I hoped that the celebration might hearten them for the struggles ahead; they'd endured hard times before. Yet it felt bittersweet. Who knew how many more anniversaries they would celebrate? I felt guilty too, as, unbeknownst to them, I had declared myself available for another call.

Working to put together a time line of our history, I'd combed through the sagging file cabinets in the office and found a cache of newsletters from the 1960s. In one, the council president had written a column reminding the congregation that they would have to assume more responsibility for running the church, Their new pastor would be spending 80 percent of his time on outreach, to bolster their declining numbers. It could have been written five years ago, when I'd started; or ten, for my predecessor, or for the two pastors before him. This congregation had been in decline for more than forty years. What had made me think I'd be the one to reverse that?

The anniversary spurred me to one more property project. We had received another windfall, this one from the son of a woman who'd been a member of Saints and Sinners so long ago that even Constance was hard pressed to place her. Though no one in the family had been connected with Saints and Sinners for years, Peter wanted to have his mother's funeral here, a homecoming to a neighborhood that held a lot of family history. He'd been very grateful, and a couple of days after the funeral he came by to thank me again. As we walked through the sanctuary, he commented appreciatively on the beautiful woodwork; I murmured agreement and then said something apologetic about the frayed carpet. He pulled out a check and said, "I think this will be enough to get you a new carpet." I choked up as I saw it was for $10,000. As I thanked him, he added, "Or spend it for anything else you think is needed."

I tucked the check into the top drawer of my desk, looking forward to sharing the good news with the Saints. The next day a handful of them met in the kitchen to put together dinner for the men's shelter. I ran downstairs with the check. Four of them were sitting around the worktable peeling potatoes while Bob stood at the big stove browning ground beef and onions. I waved the check and announced, "Everybody! Look what we got—$10,000 from Mrs. Schneider's family!"

Betty looked up with a tentative smile; the others didn't even break pace with the peelers. Martha shrugged and said flatly, "Pastor, that won't even pay for the roof repair."

A flash of anger went through me. "You're right," I said in a hard voice. "I'll just tear it up." I wheeled around and stalked out of the kitchen.

Behind me I heard Betty asking, bewildered, "What's wrong with Pastor?"

I stopped on the stairs to hear the answer. Bob said tolerantly, "Oh, she's just moody."

I stomped up the stairs to my office, slammed the door, and flung myself into my desk chair. We'd just gotten $10,000! What was wrong with these people? And moody, indeed! I fumed and then found myself dissolving in helpless laughter. We were such a mismatch, these taciturn saints and their voluble pastor. As for moody—that was an understatement, if anything, for my ricochets from overwrought enthusiasm to sulky dejection. I'd railed against their obdurate pessimism and passivity; now I recognized they'd been patient and forbearing, long-suffering even, in the face of my nagging and cheerleading. No wonder the Saints were weary. They'd been in the desert for forty years. Martha had loyally supported every one of my proposals, volunteered for every program, and worked to rally others to the latest cause; now even she was finding it hard to look on the bright side.

I reported the windfall to council and proposed that we spend the $10,000 for a new carpet. It could be our 125th anniversary gift, finished in time for the celebration. In conscience I felt compelled to report that Peter hadn't designated the gift; we could decide to use it for something else. But Martha got on board for the recarpeting as only she could; ignoring my scruples, she insisted that we were obligated to use the money for new carpet. I started to object, weakly, until she silenced me with a scowl. Council voted unanimously for the carpet.

I rallied the Saints to get it done. Steve, a Feldman in-law who was a contractor and skilled builder, agreed to manage the project, which meant removing the pews, pulling up the old carpeting, and repairing the creaky floor underneath it. Then Georgia and Charlene and I started to pore over carpet samples. I had not forgotten the dispute over the flooring in the Sunday school room, so I set about softening up the Saints. I announced on Sunday that we were considering samples, but the carpet was fifty years old, and we wouldn't be able to match it exactly. Maybe a change would be nice, I mused disingenuously. A soft gold, a deep blue: those would be lovely with our stained-glass windows. In front of me in the fourth pew, Georgia rolled her eyes; we both knew they'd never go for that.

A murmur of dismay went over the congregation. Afterwards, Steve confronted me. He was flushed with anger, I was startled to see. Ordinarily he was self-controlled, even under serious provocation. "Pastor," he began, "I've been in this church for twenty years and the carpet has always been red. And if I have anything to say about it, that's the way it always will be." I was astonished to see his eyes filling with tears of rage. Who knew he cared so much about the carpet? But without his help, we'd never get the job done. This was an ultimatum. I stammered some noncommittal answer. In response, he stabbed a finger toward the floor and declared, "Red."

Georgia and Charlene and I reviewed the samples and all exclaimed over the same one, a plush weave in a deep plum color set off with small gold chevrons. It was high quality and expensive, but steeply discounted because it was the last remnant of that design. Providentially, there was just enough of it for our project, but we'd have to act fast to get it. Charlene ran her hand over it and said wistfully, "Too bad it's not the right color." Georgia sighed in agreement and turned to some other samples.

"No, wait." I said. "This will work. It's red."

Charlene gave me a puzzled look, and Georgia huffed in annoyance.

"Really. Let's show it to the congregation on Sunday, and ask them if they like this nice *red* carpet."

Charlene looked bewildered. "But, Pastor," she said. "It's not red."

I stopped her with an outstretched palm. "From now on, we're calling this *red*. Purple is red and blue, am I right? And really, you could say this is more of a reddish plum. So, are you with me or not? *This carpet is red.*"

Charlene said doubtfully, "If you say so, Pastor."

Georgia shook her head and said, "You'll never get away with it."

"We'll see," I replied. "Now both of you, again, what color is this?"

"Red," they said.

That Sunday, I announced we'd found a red that would go with the pew cushions and stained-glass windows. After worship, the congregation came up to examine the carpet sample. Constance demurred, "It looks expensive." It was, we agreed, but we were getting it at a bargain price. As for the color, everyone agreed it was a lovely red.

At the anniversary celebration, the church was filled with friends and well-wishers, all exclaiming over the handsome new carpet. Then we adjourned to the fellowship hall for dinner, a hearty spread of chicken, gravy, dressing, mashed potatoes, and green beans. We even turned a healthy profit on the event; Martha had managed to provide that dinner for well under the $15 a head we had charged. People also responded generously with anniversary checks. We ended the year with a shortfall again, but not the record-breaking one we had predicted.

A hundred twenty-five years. My own ministry occupied only a sliver of that time line. I felt humbled by the reach of their history and honored to claim a small place in it. A little forlornly, I wondered what my ministry among them would add up to, after I had given my last sermon, said good-bye to homebound members, and emptied the manse. Soon enough, the years I'd been with the Saints would fade from memory, like the oldest names in the parish register, written in 1885 in a fine spidery hand. Much of what I had done, no doubt, would prove to have been written in water.

I imagined what I might see if I were to return for another stealth reconnaissance, this one after I had left Saints and Sinners. The flower boxes that Zoe had planted and I had tended: those plants would be left to wither and die, almost certainly, the boxes of dusty soil abandoned along the sidewalk. Gary regularly swept the front porch of the manse; when he wasn't there to attend to it, the manse's front porch would be covered with dirt blown from the park, dry leaves and litter piled up in the corners. The marquee on the corner of the building would no longer bear my name, of course; maybe it would be empty or even gone, the manse and church vacant, awaiting the developer who would retrofit it for condos.

Or maybe there would be a new name there, the next pastor's name, over the same promise: "A Warm Welcome Awaits You." Others had been predicting the demise of the congregation for decades; but George had often declared, "This congregation will close over my dead body." More than once, the Saints had come to the brink of closing and rallied to live another day, another month, another year. Too stubborn to die, I thought mordantly. Then again, maybe there was another name for it: faithfulness.

Either way, I had gone as far as I could go with the Saints. It was time to heed the promptings of my restless heart, calling me away.

# CHAPTER 13

# DAUGHTERS

It took more than a year before I summoned the resolve to make it official and finish my ministry with the Saints. I had vowed to commit to them, to break out of the pattern of short-term pastorates that had greased the skids of their decline. Now, as I imagined leaving, I felt guilty and heavyhearted. I'd stayed longer than my predecessor, if that counted for anything. Otherwise, I'd ended up exactly where he had, along with the three pastors who'd come before him—with a congregation that grew smaller every year in spite of our best efforts.

My restless heart had called me out of my first vocation as a professor, and then into my ministry at Saints and Sinners. Now I was feeling it again—boredom and apathy with the work I was doing, and a hunger and thirst for something more. I wanted to work with people who had more energy and hope, in a congregation with more active and skilled leaders. In other words, I wanted just what I had chided the Saints for wanting—a congregation with more people and more money. And I had turned sixty in 2010. If I was going to make a move, it had to be soon.

March 2011. It was St. Patrick's Day, and downstairs the Saints were preparing a boiled dinner of corned beef, cabbage, and potatoes. Then Gary called to tell me my mother had been taken to the hospital; he had followed the ambulance to the emergency room. She was unconscious, but he thought he had felt a faint squeeze when he took her hand.

I gripped the steering wheel, willing myself to focus on the road as I made my way up I-95. Was this *it*? She was eighty-five, after all. Still, I could hardly imagine it, my plucky mother struck down. It had only been eight months since she'd moved from New Jersey, clearing out and selling the house where she'd lived for fifty years, to relocate to Elysian Fields, five minutes' drive from our house in Wilmington. One of the "continuing care" places springing up all around the country, it offered independent living, assisted living, and nursing care on one rambling campus of interconnected buildings surrounded by smooth lawns and well-tended flower beds. She'd settled into her new apartment and quickly found a circle of new friends (along with a couple of boyfriends). Just last week she'd joined Good Shepherd, the church where I'd been ordained.

I loved having her closer, and we had fallen into a weekly routine that I cherished. When I drove to Wilmington on Sunday afternoons, I would stop by her cozy apartment for tea and cookies. On Mondays, my day off, I'd pick her up for errands and lunch. Was I going to lose her already? Or worse, would she survive to live out her days unable to move or speak? I swiped away the tears that were blurring my vision. She needed me, and I felt fiercely determined not to fail her.

In the emergency room, my mother lay on the gurney, the ventilator tube taped around her mouth; she was still except for the rise and fall of her chest as the ventilator pushed air into her lungs. I took her hand, her fingers limp in mine, and leaned close to call her name. Nothing. Still, I felt sure she knew I was there. The ER doctor came in with a woman wearing a long shapeless dress; she looked about my age. Her hospital badge identified her as the chaplain. My mother had suffered a stroke, the doctor explained gently. It was too early to be sure, but the scans showed a large area of damage. The chaplain put a hand on my shoulder, murmured condolences.

Mom had insisted that she didn't want extreme measures. Her living will spelled it out in detail. No feeding tubes. No dialysis. No ventilator. She had rehearsed me relentlessly and made me promise I would do what she wanted. I swallowed hard, then turned to the doctor to say she had specifically said no to a ventilator. They would withdraw it soon, he told me; they had just wanted to wait until I got there, and were there other family members? I had called my brothers; they lived in North Carolina and were working out travel arrangements. I turned back to my mother and told her I knew she did not want a ventilator; she wouldn't be left that way. Just then I felt a faint squeeze of her hand. "She can hear me!" I announced, jubilant. We watched closely and saw a slight stirring under the sheet; she was moving one leg. A couple of hours later, she was off the ventilator and sitting up. When the doctor asked her who was president, the last question in the standard assessment, she hesitated and looked at me. "Bush?"

The doctor raised a hand to keep me from answering. I ignored him.

"No, c'mon, Mom, you know this," I urged. "We both voted for him and we really like him."

"Obama," she said triumphantly.

On the stroke rehabilitation unit, she was soon walking again. Since the stroke was in the right hemisphere, her language wasn't affected, and we exulted that she still seemed herself. But I felt concerned about the gaps in her memory and the confused look that often came over her face. After she was discharged from the hospital, she moved to the "health-care center" at Elysian Fields, which had a highly rated stroke-rehabilitation program. When I went into her old apartment to gather some clothes, my breath caught as I saw the quilt squares laid out on her bed, the quilt top she had been assembling when she'd had the stroke. She was determined to go back there, and I too held on to the hope that she'd return to independent living.

She had daily physical therapy to improve her strength and balance, and help her compensate for "left-sided inattention"; she tended to list off course when navigating down the hall, or overlook objects in that part of her visual field. Then there were the drills and tasks to recover or remap the neural connections scrambled by the stroke. I was taken aback by what these revealed. Mom could tell time, but she was repeatedly defeated as she tried to draw a clock face. The therapist laid out her efforts like an indictment; the numbers were jumbled in a heap on the right, or out of order, set in a wavering circle or lopsided oval.

Mom was chagrined to realize she was making mistakes on these kindergarten tasks, but increasingly she was impatient with the therapy—and the therapist. Joanne was tall and heavyset, her faded blond hair loosely gathered into a lopsided bun. With Mom she was patient but firm, prodding her through exercises of memory and analytic skills. When I came by to visit after one session, Mom made a face and confided in a loud whisper, "I don't like her." Asked yet again to produce a clock face, she protested, "What's the difference? Who needs to draw a clock?" I laughed when Joanne reported this to me, but she took it as evidence for the prosecution: "She lacks insight into her condition, typical of right-hemisphere damage." I asked how she thought Mom was doing, when she would be able to go back to her apartment. She shook her head. "She won't. Assisted living, eventually."

Walking down the hall with her one day, I heard someone behind me saying in a low voice, "Is that the daughter?" That was me, and I struggled to rise to the occasion. On my Mondays in Wilmington I scrambled to keep up: laundry, bills, mail, conferences with her caregivers. During the week Gary visited her while I worked at Saints and Sinners. I delayed as long as I could on bigger decisions, hoping she could take over herself. Some days she could manage writing a check, with my coaching her through each line as she railed against the bills. She had always been very "careful" with money, as she put it. Now her long habit of thrift had morphed into outsized anxiety about money.

Whether it was a $20 charge for a newspaper subscription or the $4,000 tab for a month at Elysian Fields, she reviewed every bill with gasps of dismay and then declared, "I'm not paying for that."

So I fished out the power of attorney she had executed years ago. But when I took the yellowed paperwork to the bank, the officer shook her head and let me know that it was no good. I found a lawyer and explained my dilemma. He told me what to do, even as he warned that he wouldn't execute the power of attorney unless he was convinced my mother was competent to grant it. I wanted to weep in frustration at the catch-22. I held my breath when I brought her to his office to review the documents. She struggled to focus, asked a few questions, and nodded gravely when he asked if she understood and wanted to sign. He gave me a brisk nod—she had passed—and she signed the documents to move her assets into a trust and name me as cotrustee. Afterwards, she sagged with fatigue and thanked me tearfully.

I felt pierced as my mother became more dependent on me, even as I was deeply glad to care for her. When I left her at Elysian Fields after a visit, she always came to the door to wave good-bye. One day two of her friends came with her, both frail and unsteady; they clung to my slightly sturdier mother, one on each side. As she thanked me, one of them exclaimed, "What would we do without our daughters?" The others chorused, "Yes, what would we do without our daughters?" I smiled through tears, weary but grateful to be my mother's daughter.

By the end of 2011, my plan to leave Saints and Sinners was official but not yet public. I had told the bishop I wanted to be considered for another call and submitted the paperwork used to match pastors and congregations. I hadn't yet told any of the Saints; the process was supposed to remain confidential until the pastor announced an impending departure on a specific date. This transitional state felt awkward. I didn't want to start new projects when I was unlikely to see them through, and yet I also didn't want to let them go from stall to free fall. And I still sometimes felt torn myself, subject to the occasional relapse into delusions of staying on to save them.

Mostly, I felt relieved to imagine leaving, and energized by the prospect of a new congregation. I expected to work for another ten or fifteen years, eager for a congregation that gave me more scope to use my experience in teaching and writing and working with young adults. I felt a stirring of anticipation when I opened the large envelopes containing profiles of congregations that the bishop's assistant was inviting me to consider. A couple of them I declined. They seemed just like Saints and Sinners: congregations with barely enough money and energy to keep going. Others seemed like places I could imagine going. I went to interviews in northern Virginia and the eastern shore of Maryland, in southern Delaware, and two that were near our home in Wilmington. I got to the last stage in four of them, only to be disappointed when another candidate got the call.

My heart sinking, I began to realize I might not get a new call. Small and struggling congregations hoped for a young pastor. Often, what they wanted was a young man, preferably with a wife and small children, who would attract more young families and stay for years, the way some pastor of beloved memory had done. Though in reality I was likely to stay longer than the newly graduated first-call pastor they would probably get, it was also incontrovertibly true that I would not be there for twenty years or more. The larger congregations were looking for someone more experienced (and younger). And all of them wanted someone who could lead a youth ministry, whether or not they actually had any youth to lead. Whatever assets I might bring to the table, I was also female, sixty, and with a first call in a congregation that had steadily declined on my watch.

I went to a daylong retirement seminar with a couple of dozen other pastors. The leader, dressed in a crisp oxford blouse and a navy blazer, was a financial-planning specialist hired by our benefits association. After a brisk review of the agenda, she posed the crucial first question: How long are you going to live? She waited out our laughter and mordant comments and continued. Yes, of course no one could be certain of that, but we had to set a parameter. One in five of us would live well into our nineties, she advised, setting off murmurs of consternation. Next to me, a male colleague nudged me and whispered, "That's you, Barbara." "God forbid," I answered fervently. For three hours we were barraged with information on annuities, long-term-care insurance, Social Security, pensions, and balanced financial portfolios. The session ended with a questionnaire to assess our "readiness for retirement," along with a daunting to-do list for the well-planned segue to golden-years unemployment.

At home I consulted the "mortality calculators" she had told us to check. My colleague was right; I was on target to make it to ninety-eight, or ninety-nine if I improved my attitude (I got a year knocked off for "negative views of aging"). I couldn't fathom a retirement of close to forty years, let alone leaving ministry after a first call that turned out to be my last call. And yet, as my prospects for a new call dwindled, it seemed I had joined the ranks of people who were too young (or so we believed) to retire, but too old to get another job.

But forget the to-do list for retirement; I had all I could do to keep up at Saints and Sinners while managing Mom's care. Finally an apartment had opened up in assisted living, and we'd moved her things from her old apartment. I was relieved to get her out of the health-care center, where most of the residents spent their days slumped in wheelchairs positioned along the halls.

But her less restricted life in new quarters had its downside too. When I went to meet her on Mondays, I usually found her apartment empty and had to undertake a search through the warren of connected buildings. She could read a clock face but couldn't understand what it meant to meet at a specific time. Then there was the day she went AWOL; the director of assisted living called me to report she'd gone missing for a couple of hours, spirited off by some male resident in his car. The perp was never identified; she had either forgotten his name or wouldn't give him up. I murmured with feigned concern but was secretly amused.

But I was shaken by reports of her waking in the night, disoriented and agitated, wandering the halls in her nightgown. A few months ago I'd been determined to help her get back to independent living; now I was afraid she might flunk out of assisted living and end up back in the health-care unit or, worse, be consigned to "memory care," the locked ward for patients with severe dementia.

Fall 2011. Even as Mom was faltering with age, Amy was being overtaken by the cancer that had interrupted her life. By the numbers, she had hit the oncology lottery more than once. We had celebrated last summer, when she cleared the one-year survival mark. Then she defied the odds again for a second year, and through most of it she had been able to keep up ordinary routines and take care of her bubbly preschooler. They had even added a puppy to the mix, Honey, a feckless golden retriever whose antics wreaked havoc on the house and yard. But now the cancer was rebounding, and the chemo was flattening her.

When I visited her at home one afternoon, she met me at the door, then half collapsed back onto the couch. We shared Communion and afterwards I prayed, searching for words that would tell the truth about this mortal struggle. Courage, I asked for, and trust, in the face of things we could not understand. I added, "God, you know everything in our hearts: the fear, the doubt, the anger." At "anger," Amy let out a murmur of agreement. So I ventured, "It's got to be so hard for you, wondering if you're going to be here to see Grace grow up." But that was too much. She turned her head away and closed her eyes, saying, "I have to rest now."

December. For Christmas Eve we were doing "Christmas in Song and Story," featuring lessons and carols interspersed with scenes from a children's pageant. I had premiered this service last year and the Saints had loved it. This year I wanted to take it over the top, knowing this was likely my last Christmas Eve with them. Wayside Stage had lent us a spotlight, installed it in the choir loft, and coached one of the Saints on the lighting script. A couple of mothers of the cast were helping to stage and direct; one of them had ordered angel costumes with gold tinsel haloes and white net wings sparkly with glitter and rhinestones. We had tiaras and Burger King crowns for the magi (who would include both boys and girls in my nontraditional casting).

As always, it was a challenge to get the kids together for rehearsals, with harried parents racing against the calendar in the countdown to Christmas. When I did manage to assemble them, it was like herding kittens. I did have one rock-solid trouper, Grace's cousin David. He was eight years old with a gravitas that belied his years; he had demonstrated his chops in last year's pageant, and I had appointed him head shepherd this year. I had no doubt that he would get his junior shepherds where they needed to be, along with the winsome four-year-old we were squeezing into an adorable sheep costume (with luck it would still fit by Christmas).

The angels, though, were another matter. These roles would be played by Grace, her cousin Lily (David's younger sister), and Melanie (she and her mother had recently joined). They had the crucial scene, and I was not sure they were up to it. The three were supposed to leap from stage left on "tidings of great joy," flutter to center stage, then raise their arms together at "Glory to God in the highest heaven." Ideally, they would beam with jubilant smiles at this point; or at least, I hoped, not become unhinged with stage fright. Grace was the youngest, barely five years old, but she listened and watched with quiet intensity as I coached the actors on their lines and cues. Grace knew her stuff, and I thought she could deliver the angels on Christmas Eve.

It was a flimsy plan, counting on a five-year-old to carry the show, and not just any five-year-old, but one whose mother was gravely ill. If Amy died right before Christmas, this whole pageant was going down; Gracie and her two cousins would be home with their grieving families, and I'd be down two angels and a shepherd. The irony of it was not lost on me. Here I was, fretting over a children's play even as Amy's life was leaking away. But pageants have their place, and I accounted this as one of the unexpected blessings of pastoral work, this juxtaposition of ordinary and ultimate things. So the show would go on, or not.

Christmas Eve. Amy was too sick to get to church, but she insisted that everyone else should go. As the church began to fill up, we lit the tall candles on the ends of the pews. The ushers dimmed the lights, the congregation fell into a hush of anticipation, and the show was on. I held my breath as the angels' entrance approached. Right on cue, Gracie led the other angels to center stage. At "Glory to God," the three raised their arms together, beaming with delight as Marie struck up a few bars of the Alleluia chorus. Gracie's face was radiant in the soft light, rapt with concentration. The light glinted off their haloes. The congregation stirred with sighs of appreciation, and I heard a few soft sniffles.

As the new year began, I resolved to set a date for my departure, even as I felt stricken about leaving Amy and her family in this mortal anguish. Barbara raged and grieved. How could God take away her daughter, and a daughter who was herself a mother? I had hoped to see it through, as I put it to myself, but in effect that meant waiting for her to die. And that wouldn't be the end for her family, not for Daniel or for Gracie, not for her parents or brother and sister. I would always be leaving in the middle of something; that was the nature of congregational life. I had not planned to leave the Saints without a new call, but it wasn't fair to stay when my heart wasn't in it anymore.

So it was time to go public, to tell the council and leadership, followed by a letter to the whole congregation. I started draft after draft, and imagined myself delivering the news to council, to George and Constance, to Martha and Georgia. Then I'd also have to visit all our homebound people to say good-bye. I dreaded it all, and I couldn't seem to find my way to the words I would need to say and write. My attempts kept devolving into self-justification and blame, as if toads and snakes were leaping out of my mouth unbidden. "I've done everything I could do with the help of a few people, but without more commitment . . ." "We've seen some encouraging growth these last few years, but I find myself doing more and more of the ministry that belongs to all of us." "I have learned from you and grown with you; now, though, I want to find a call where my gifts of teaching and writing will be more fully used" (snarky pastor-speak for "You don't appreciate me, so I'm done"). When I auditioned these efforts with Gary, he vetoed one after the other. "No. This is not the time to instruct them. They won't hear it anyway." It had to be short, he declared. One sentence.

While I struggled to find that sentence, I met with the bishop to work out the details. Except in unusual circumstances, pastors did not depart right before Christmas or Easter. I also needed to coordinate my announcement with the bishop's assistant's calendar; right after I told the congregation I was leaving, a representative of the synod would meet with council to help them through the transition. A month's notice was good, but it shouldn't be much longer—enough time to wrap things up, without lingering. So we agreed I'd tell the congregation the third week in March, and leave on May 1.

With the timetable in place, I had to get my script in order. "Just say you have to take care of your mother," Gary said. "People will understand that." I didn't want to blame her, or to admit that I was frazzled and worn out as I ratcheted between pastoral duties and a "day off" consumed by errands and appointments. But he was right; the Saints would accept that reason. And it was the truth, if not the whole truth. I was the daughter, and my mother needed me.

But Mom wasn't going to let me get away with that. On March 6 I got a call from the nursing director at Elysian Fields. She reported that Mom had been up all night vomiting, and the nurse on duty was worried about her breathing. She had begged them not to send her to the emergency room and told them fiercely, "Don't call my daughter! I'll be fine!" But by morning she looked worse, and they had sent her to the ER.

Gary went to the ER to see her and called me to report that the doctors had found nothing serious. He reported wryly that Mom kept apologizing, insisting, "I told them not to call you! I'm such a nuisance. Go home!" So he had, leaving her in the ER to wait for a bed; they were planning to keep her overnight, just in case. A couple of hours later, he sent an e-mail to let me know he had checked with the ER again and she was fine, still waiting for a room. As I was reading the message again, the phone rang. So I was confused, and protested at first, when Gary said gently, "Your mother died." She had gone into cardiac arrest on the ER gurney.

After seven years at Saints and Sinners, I had logged many hours in funeral homes and done more than fifty funerals. But I'd never been the one making the arrangements. It felt both familiar and raw, this ritual of getting the dead and the living where we needed to go. I summoned my brothers and their families, found a funeral director, called the hospital to release her body. The next day Gary and I went to the funeral home in Wilmington; I'd never been in this one, but it was reassuringly familiar all the same, with its plush pale-blue carpeting and dark furniture. In the office the funeral director slid price lists in front of me, options for memorial cards, guest books, obituaries. Next, he took us to the showroom to select the container for her ashes. And then it was time to identify her body before it went into the furnace. I felt that steely calm that came over me under stress. Down the hall and through double doors into a long empty room. Against one wall, framed by pink torch lights, her body lay under a sheet pulled up to her chin. Gary stood next to me for a long moment as we looked down at her, then squeezed my hand and stepped back to wait outside.

Her softly curled hair was brushed back from her forehead. Death had smoothed out the fine lines that had creased her face. Her lips, still full, were pale and a little chapped. I had been upset to hear they'd attempted resuscitation in the ER. In all likelihood she would not have been aware of it, but still I hated to think of it, the team crowded around her, one to tip back her head to place a breathing tube, another to hold the shock paddles to her chest, the order "Stand clear!" as the voltage went through her and her body jumped. Leaning closer, I was relieved to see that the intubation in the ER had not abraded her mouth. I pulled the sheet back a little and glanced at her chest—no bruising. As I had hoped, they had probably made only token efforts to resuscitate her.

Then I covered her body and leaned over to cup her face in my hands. So familiar, that beloved face, even as this body was so clearly uninhabited. I had come out of that body. Was I still her daughter, or anyone's daughter, now that both my parents were dead? Her skin was soft, her flesh yielding under my palms, but cold, so cold. I found myself pressing my hands more firmly around her cheeks, as if to warm them. Tears welled in my eyes and spilled down my cheeks.

But that lifeless body wasn't her, and it wasn't even hers anymore. The dead own nothing. Her body belonged to me now, but it was mine only to return to dust and ashes. I turned and walked away without looking back.

# CHAPTER 14

## LEAVE-TAKING

Ashes to ashes. The cherrywood cube held what was left of my mother, a reminder of mortality that braced me like a brisk wind on a cold bright day, exhilarating and monitory. I set the container on the passenger seat next to me, oddly comforted by the thought that Mom was riding shotgun once more. On the day of the funeral I held her ashes in my lap as Gary drove to Good Shepherd, and then placed them on a table next to the baptismal font.

My heart filled as I looked around at the fifty or so people gathered here: my family, longtime friends, members of Good Shepherd, and a few people from Baltimore. My mother's best friend Shirley from New Jersey had come, along with a little group of newer friends from Elysian Fields. Mom had joined Good Shepherd just a week before her stroke, so she hadn't attended regularly for a while. But the congregation had gathered around her, and us. I felt warmed as I looked around and saw people I'd known for more than twenty years, when Gary and I had found harbor at Good Shepherd. My ministry at Saints and Sinners had started here with my ordination seven years ago; now I had come nearly full circle.

I hadn't expected the Saints to show up. It was short notice, and Wilmington was unknown territory for most, the Monday redoubt of their pastor but otherwise not on the map of their intimate geography. But three members had ventured the trip from Baltimore; Renee and Scott had carpooled with Kathleen. Ellen and Bill filled out the Baltimore contingent, their faces somber. Constance and George had been a steady presence at nearly every funeral I had done; today they were absent, but Constance had called several times to offer support and to let me know they were taking care of things while I was away.

Pastor Kathy greeted us at the front, her purple stole laid over a neatly pressed alb, her face ringed with dark curls. I had done so many funerals, more than fifty; I felt grateful that this time, someone else would gather the family and say the prayers and give the sermon. Today it was my turn to mourn and to be lifted up by the church's language of lament and hope.

Two days later I was back at Saints and Sinners, and it was time to take leave of them. I couldn't say now that my mother needed me. In the end, I simply said, "It's time." I told Constance first. She looked stricken, and I felt miserable to be the cause of her distress. Then she said haltingly, "I didn't realize you were unhappy." I hadn't expected that. Constance was an astute observer, and I had feared my frustration was all too evident. If it hadn't been obvious to her, probably others hadn't noticed either; maybe that meant I had put up a better front than I knew. But how could she not have seen how much it had cost me, these years of struggle?

And "unhappy"? What was with that? It was true enough, of course, but happiness was too personal—and too trivial—a metric for ministry or call. Constance herself, as far as I knew, did not aspire to anything so superficial as happiness. But this was not the time to try to justify myself or explain. I felt suddenly reminded of every breakup I'd ever initiated, and fell back on the only gracious exit line I knew: "It isn't you, it's me."

I told Ellen next. She murmured sympathetically; she'd been my partner in ministry since she'd first become our administrative assistant, and we'd become friends. Then she turned away, trying to hide her tears. I went over to hug her, and we held on to each other for a long moment. And then back to work. The letter had to go out that day, so that it would reach the congregation before Sunday.

I'd called a special meeting of council. They gathered in the parlor looking wary. At my announcement, a murmur of dismay went around the room. Georgia looked grim and said, "I knew it." She'd guessed that I might be planning a move when she'd seen the stuff piled high on the manse porch, things I'd purged and set out for Goodwill. Chuck maintained the poker face that was the family specialty and said matter-of-factly, "Well, time to organize another call committee." He'd been a member of the committee that had called me, and veteran of all too many pastorates; now I had joined the list of those who had come and gone.

I went to Barbara and Mel's house to tell them. Barbara answered the door and wrapped me in an embrace, offering condolences for my mother's death. We stepped over toys in their cozy front room; they looked after Gracie and her cousins most afternoons. I sat across from them on the couch, sinking into the battered brown cushions. They both looked worn, slumped with fatigue and grief. In January the doctors had stopped the chemo; it wasn't working, only making Amy sicker. Mel and Amy had thrown themselves into a determined search for clinical trials, but the protocols were exacting, and she was rejected for one after another.

When I told them I was leaving in six weeks, they accepted it as one more bit of bad news, minor by comparison to what they were facing. Gracious as always, they asked how I was doing, back at work with my mother's death so fresh. As I got up to leave, Barbara leaned forward and took my hands, thanking me for being their pastor and wishing me happiness in whatever came next. I managed to stumble down the steps and onto the broken sidewalk before I started sobbing.

I brought Communion to Amy. It was a raw March day, overcast and damp; I could smell the wet earth. Along the sidewalk leading to their house, hyacinths had poked through the ground, their spiky buds still furled tight. Amy had planted them in the fall; now, she could hardly get to the front door to let me in. She winced and gave a weary sigh as she arranged pillows to support her on the couch. The light had gone out of her face. Pale, almost gray, skin stretched over her cheekbones. I tentatively brought up the D word, but even though by then she must have known it was coming, she didn't want to talk about death. She went silent, then told me that she and Gracie were decorating a hat for Grace to wear with her new Easter dress.

I got three condolence cards from the staff and CEO of Elysian Fields, followed by a crisp business letter announcing that my mother's apartment had to be cleared out in three weeks. I felt pierced. Not so long ago, we had been impatiently awaiting just such an event to befall someone else, even as I'd felt guiltily aware that a vacancy in assisted living meant that someone had slid down to the health-care unit or made their final exit. Now my mother's death had opened up one of those coveted spaces.

With Holy Week looming, I hired someone to help me pack up her stuff and found a mover who would make two stops to deliver some of it to my brothers. I opened her drawers and cupboard and the closet in her bedroom, taking the measure of what was left. When the movers had driven off, I took a few loads out to the car: a couple of small lamps, the small mirror she'd hung near the door, photo albums, towels, and sheets. I set aside her flowered teapot; I would give that to Shirley, a memento of the many afternoons they'd shared tea at my mother's kitchen table in New Jersey. I took a few of her sweaters and tops for myself. Then I swept the floor and scrubbed out the kitchen, took one last look around, locked the door, and left the key at the office.

Holy Week. As always, it was taxing, the annual overload of a week with four or five sermons to prepare, three special bulletins, two changes of the paraments, and the seasonal ordeal of the lily supplement. Everyone who gave a lily was acknowledged in the Easter bulletin and in that month's *Herald Angel*. That meant checking and rechecking to make sure we hadn't left anyone out, proofreading the names, and lining them up in the correct columns: "In honor of" for the living and "In memory of" for the dead. The hectoring details swarmed like gnats—the palms for the procession on Palm Sunday; the basin and towel for Holy Thursday foot washing; the candelabras and rough-hewn cross for Good Friday; the extra chalices for Communion on Easter Sunday. And oh yes, I had said I would bake the bread. So Holy Week was wearing, and at the same time extravagantly, almost unbearably, rich, this week marked by the rhythms of ancient liturgies, strange and compelling.

This year, Holy Week was freighted with the anticipation of loss. I was flooded with memories of that first Holy Week seven years ago, when I had started my ministry at Saints and Sinners on Palm Sunday. I smiled and winced to remember how I had floundered through it, camping out in the manse and new to everything. Now I was moving through these rituals for the last time here— and maybe for the last time ever, I thought bleakly, with no new call on the horizon.

Since I had decided to leave, every occasion was charged with that sense of ending. Sometimes I was relieved, even giddy. Done with difficult council meetings! Sometimes I was sad; this last month, I had been visiting homebound members to say good-bye. Sometimes I was sucked into that vortex of "if only," rehearsing my frustrations again, and filled with a sense of failure. Sometimes I felt filled to the brim with the gifts of these years: the deep relationships, the place I had held in this community, the unexpected blessing of it all. Regret, anger, weariness; and gratitude, wonder, love. Bittersweet.

On Wednesday morning of Holy Week, I was in my study when Barbara called, her voice thick with tears. Amy had just died at home. In the next room, the copy machine was thumping out pages for the bulletins. Ellen looked up as I opened the door between our offices. "Amy," she said when she saw my face, and got up to embrace me. I hurried to the manse to pull on a clergy shirt, my fingers fumbling with the studs as I attached the collar. Barbara was waiting on the corner a few blocks down. I got out of the car to hold her close and felt her chest and shoulders heaving as we both cried. When I pulled up in front of Amy and Daniel's house and got out, the spicy scent of hyacinths filled the air, the pink and purple and white stalks lining the front path. Daniel was waiting at the open front door, his face blank, his eyes red and circled with dark shadows. In their bedroom, Amy lay with her eyes closed, the covers pulled up over her chest. Her face was smooth, wiped of pain and fear. Her oxygen had been turned off but the plastic cannulae were still in her nose, the tubing draped over her chest and arm. I felt a sudden urgency to get rid of it, this apparatus of illness, useless now and somehow a violation of her still body. I started to take it off, then stopped to ask Daniel if that was OK. When he nodded slightly, I loosened the slide under her chin and took the prongs from her nose, then balled up the tubing and stuffed it out of sight between the bed and the nightstand. Her arm rolled off the side of the mattress; startled, I caught it on my thigh. It was shockingly heavy, like a sandbag. Dead weight: the cliché took on sudden vivid meaning. I put her arm back on the bed, snugging it closer to her body. Mel arrived, then Amy's sister and brother. We stood in a circle around Amy's body as I said the commendation of the dying, one hand on her shoulder. At the end I traced a cross on her forehead; under my thumb her skin was already cool.

We stepped away from her body and turned to the rituals that surrounded a death. Daniel called the funeral home. Others pulled out their cell phones to notify others Amy had died. Grace was with Arlene, off visiting other relatives. They were an hour's ride away, and no one wanted to think of Arlene driving right after hearing the news; it would come soon enough, when they were safely off the road. I went into the kitchen to get some water. On the refrigerator door, I saw the letter I'd sent Amy, the Bible verses she'd requested, words to sustain her in the pain and fear and uncertainty of this abyss.

An unmarked white van pulled up in front of the house, and two men in dark suits got out. The folded-up gurney rattled over the sidewalk. Barbara took Amy's cat and Honey into the back yard, and sat on the back step; the others followed her outside. Daniel led the men into the bedroom; I stepped aside and stood in the hall outside the room. With efficient motions, they rolled Amy's body from one side and then the other, tucking the shroud underneath and then wrapping it over her body. The black body bag lay open on the gurney. They scooped their arms under her and lifted her body onto the gurney, then zipped up the bag. Daniel followed them as they wheeled the gurney out of the room, into the short hall, and out the front door. I watched as they bumped it down the front steps and along the sidewalk lined with hyacinths. Across the street a curtain flicked open; maybe a neighbor had noticed the unfamiliar cars and then this van. The men lifted the gurney into the van, slammed and latched the doors. As they drove away, Daniel sank to the top step and dropped his head into his hands.

Easter. The church was not full, even on this Sunday of all Sundays, not anymore. White Easter lilies flanked the altar, set on rickety wooden tiers; other clusters of lilies, all in gold-foil wrapped pots, were arranged around the reading stand and the pulpit. I breathed in the heavy sweet scent and reminded myself not to brush against them; another Easter, the powdery pollen on those deep yellow stamens had set an indelible stain on the hem of my alb. After we'd prayed in the sacristy, the acolyte went out to light the candles, and the assisting minister and I went down the side aisle to line up for the procession.

The congregation rose for the opening hymn as we followed the cross down the center aisle, voices swelling around us, "Jesus Christ Is Risen Today." At the front I turned around, and saw them coming in to fill a whole pew in the back: Barbara and Mel, where they usually sat, along with Amy's brother, her sister and husband and their two kids, Lily and David. Daniel looked shaky but resolute. Grace stood on the pew next to him, her eyes wide and face rosy under her Easter hat.

Two days later, the church was filled for the funeral. Amy's family was seated in the front pews; Daniel's parents were behind them, looking worn and ill at ease. I went over to Barbara and kneeled next to her, gripping her hands, then greeted the rest of the family. I nodded to Marie, who started playing the piano while I lit the candles on the altar and then the tall candle next to the baptismal font. I walked down the side aisle to the back, where the white coffin nearly filled the narthex. George lifted the ivory silk pall from the back pew, and he and I placed it over the coffin, a familiar ritual by now—and this time, another last thing.

I squeezed past the coffin to pry the processional cross from its clamp on the wall. The funeral home attendants turned the coffin carefully in the narrow space. As I started down the aisle with the cross, I could hear the wheels of the gurney creaking behind me. At the front I stepped well back so the men could turn the coffin again and set it across the front, the head next to the font. Then I lifted a pitcher of water high and poured it into the metal bowl. At funerals we come back to the water of baptism, where we drown and are reborn: death and resurrection.

For the readings, I used the ones that I had given Amy, from my copy of the sheet she'd put on her refrigerator. Gary came to the lectern and began to read, his deep voice weighting the words from Joshua: "I hereby command you: Be strong and courageous; do not be frightened or dismayed, for the Lord your God is with you wherever you go." Then Zoe followed, her clear precise voice and poet's ear attuned to the cadences of biblical poetry. "Be still, and know that I am God." "The Lord is my strength and my shield." "When you pass through the waters, I will be with you; and through the rivers, they shall not overwhelm you." Gary finished with the ringing oratory of Paul in Romans 8: "For I am convinced that neither death, nor life, nor angels, nor rulers, nor things present, nor things to come, nor powers, nor height, nor depth, nor anything else in all creation, will be able to separate us from the love of God in Christ Jesus our Lord." These ancient words, ever renewed as they are heard again in new circumstances, at once transcendent and intimately personal. I was filled with the words; steadied too to hear them spoken by Gary and Zoe, standing side by side, somber and composed, these two who had been support and joy to me through this and so much more.

I'd felt gutted writing the sermon. In it I evoked the memory of their wedding in this place, that day of celebration not quite six years ago. Amy and Daniel had chosen the beloved passage from 1 Corinthians 13: "Love bears all things, believes all things, hopes all things, endures all things." These words, worn smooth by familiarity, sounded stark as I read them now, with the coffin in front of us bearing witness to what love had been called to bear.

I spoke directly to Daniel, weeping in the front pew, asking if he remembered my challenge to them on their wedding day. I had started my sermon with a playful but pointed question, asking each in turn, "Are you ready for this?" No one is, not really. A marriage covenant is a blank check if ever there was one, for who knows what will come? Joys and griefs that cannot be foreseen, that we do not dare even imagine. When I acknowledge this uncertainty in a wedding sermon, my prediction hardly counts as prophecy; of course we do not know what lies ahead, or how we will meet or falter before life's trials.

Still, as I stood to preach with Amy's coffin before me, my wedding sermon echoed like an ominous portent. Around the room I saw many people who had been here to witness their marriage promises, and who had come now to grieve. And those wedding vows — "in sickness and in health" and "'til death do us part" — are solemn promises, words to sober even the most reckless of young lovers; but no one who had heard Amy and Daniel make those pledges would have suspected they would come due so soon. Daniel certainly had not expected that he would be the one to redeem the somber blessing of a marriage that endures until death, that so soon after their wedding, he would grieve at her grave.

Before the wedding, Amy and Daniel had come to me for premarital counseling, or "marriage preparation" as we called it — a rash claim at best. They'd been game, dutifully completing the workbook I assigned and showing up for the five appointed sessions. The last session was one that left most couples utterly stymied. It was an invitation to imagine the future, complete with a worksheet with boxes to fill in; two years, five years, fifteen, and twenty-five years, what might their life together be, at those removes? Daniel had shrugged and declared the future unfathomable, leaving his worksheet blank. But Amy had filled hers with neat writing. They were already planning to buy a house; maybe they'd save enough for a second one later on, a little place at the beach. In a couple of years, a first child; then another, a few years after that. She had pondered what the years might bring for their families: their children growing up and going off to college or work; their parents aging and maybe needing help; their own retirements; their children's marriages; becoming grandparents.

Cancer hadn't figured in the plan.

I started to waver, my mouth trembling a little. I gripped the sides of the reading desk and looked away from the wet faces in the front pews, took a ragged breath, and went on. Amy wanted passionately to live. I remembered her fierce resolve in the consultation room that first day, as the diagnosis loomed: "If it is cancer, I'm going to kick its ass." If courage and determination and endurance were enough, I declared, then Amy would be among us still. And what of all our prayers? God had not intervened to save her, not as we'd hoped, anyway. But God had suffered with her, and showed up wherever love had sustained her and all of them in this time of trial. For some, no doubt, that proclamation rang hollow, maybe even called forth a bitter disavowal. But I said it anyway. I believed it. And it was my job to be hopeful, to hold fast to Jesus' own promise of abundant life.

The cemetery was forty minutes' drive from the church, and I sank back into the big padded seat of the hearse, grateful for a little respite. When we turned off the highway into the cemetery grounds, the long line of cars snaked behind the hearse to the grave.

I got out with the funeral director and waited as people spilled from their cars and made their way over the grass. I squinted at the light; it was a brilliantly sunny day, the air sweet with apple and cherry blossoms. I stepped back as the funeral director swung open the back doors of the hearse, arranged the pallbearers in two lines, and directed them to pick up the coffin as it slid from the hearse's rails. Then I stepped in front of the coffin and slowly led the procession to the grave; when I arrived, I turned to watch the pallbearers as they lurched over the uneven ground.

*Occasional Services* fell open to the page for burial of the dead; these last seven years, I had used this rite more than any other. Now I spoke the familiar words over Amy's grave: "Almighty God, by the death and burial of Jesus, your anointed, you have destroyed death and sanctified the graves of all your saints." Then the strange triumphant invocation from Paul: "For the trumpet will sound, and the dead will be raised imperishable, and we shall be changed." The commendation, "earth to earth, ashes to ashes, dust to dust." The invitation to pray the Lord's Prayer, and the blessing. "Let us go in peace," I concluded, and the crowd around the grave began to disperse, moving slowly through the cemetery to the place for the funeral lunch.

When I reached the building, I turned back and looked toward the grave. The coffin was still suspended over it, covered with a huge spray of flowers. A cemetery worker in a tan jumpsuit was pulling up the thin carpet of fake grass that had concealed the raw earth. Then off to the side in a stand of trees I saw something stirring: the backhoe, inching from behind the trees to fill her grave.

# EPILOGUE

# A PIECE OF MY HEART

I was supposed to stay away from the congregation after I left. It was better that way, I knew. The Saints had to be set free to welcome a new pastor with undivided hearts. Still, I found myself drawn back, straining to catch a glimpse of the church from the highway when I drove past Baltimore on the interstate. It was tantalizingly just out of sight — screened by a high wall to dampen the highway noise. One day, I gave in to temptation and took the exit into the neighborhood. Another stealth reconnaissance, like the one Gary and I had undertaken when I'd been considering this call, more than seven years ago. This time, I wouldn't risk getting out of the car.

The main street through the neighborhood looked the same, with scraggly trees parched in the late August heat. When I got to Saints and Sinners, I saw that the flower boxes were filled with dead plants, and litter was piled under the overgrown bushes. Six-foot thistles flanked the office entrance; more than once, I'd pulled them up only to find a new crop there within weeks. The new pastor's name was on the marquee; this time, the Saints had scored a young man, recently married. The manse porch looked dusty behind the wrought-iron gate, with a couple of battered lawn chairs set out. I felt a grudging approval; it seemed the new pastor had taken on the local custom of sitting on the front steps. The welcome banner over the church door was holding up, and a colorful new banner was stretched along one wall, announcing a new community garden in the manse yard.

Every month when the *Herald Angel* arrived in the mail, I tore it open and scrutinized each sentence for the real news, what hints of it I could glean from the spare minutes of council meetings or the lists of prayer concerns. In his monthly columns, the pastor touted his new initiatives for outreach, declaring that the congregation was finally beginning to connect with the neighborhood. I felt stung. Did he think I'd done nothing there? But it was none of my business now. Besides, I recognized an echo of my own exhortations in his words. I too had underestimated the efforts of those who had come before me, and had set to work with a reckless overconfidence in what I could do to change things. Now I had to let it go, to make peace with what I had done and left undone.

What did that amount to, the seven years I'd spent with the Saints? If I had accomplished anything of lasting value, it had left no traces on our membership rolls or our balance sheets. The congregation was smaller than when I had started, and our finances more precarious. The fresh paint, new carpets, and incursions against clutter counted for something—or so I told myself—but they would soon enough be undone.

As for the programs I'd promoted or the meetings I'd led, the door hangers I'd distributed, or the newsletter columns I'd written, if any of that had mattered, I could not see it. I had not been successful, not by the metrics of church growth and renewal, not by the measure of my own ambitions and aspirations.

I had not been successful, but I had been faithful. I had showed up at Saints and Sinners, and I'd become their pastor by joining them in the rhythms of congregational life. The bread and wine I had blessed, week after week; the longing and gratitude and grief I'd seen in their faces as I placed bread in their hands. The words spoken and sung,

the whispered prayers and silent tears. The hours I'd labored to prepare for preaching, and the rich full silence that sometimes followed
a sermon. The water I'd poured into the font, the silver shell I'd used
to scoop the water over a new Christian. The pattern of the church
year—Advent, Christmas, Epiphany, Lent, Easter, and Pentecost,
and the long green season of Ordinary Time. The sacraments of the
fellowship hall: spaghetti dinners, tag sales, pancakes and sausage.

I had not been successful, but I'd been blessed—blessed in ordinary things, and in unexpected places. A nursing-home vigil. The
jazz concert on that hot night. Singing karaoke with the Saints.
After a funeral, watching the pallbearers as they carried a coffin to
the grave, and blessing the people who gathered to grieve there. In
these places, I'd truly known the Saints, and been known by them.
I'd been lit by grace. And I'd met Jesus where he was always to be
found: hidden in the ordinary, revealed in the unexpected.

Even now I sometimes take a detour that brings me back to
Saints and Sinners. What draws me there, I wonder? What is it
that I'm looking for? Maybe it is a little bit like first love, this first
call; I'd left a piece of my heart with the Saints. Or maybe that's
the way of my restless heart, forever seeking what is already mine.

I have written this book over many years, and over those years my
own sense of ministry and call have changed. Much of that story is
told in these pages. Here is what happened after I left Saints and
Sinners.

I went back to Wilmington without a call. A local congregation
invited me to apply for a part-time hourly job as a pastoral associ-
ate; after I was interviewed, the congregation decided to use the
money for a vicar, a seminary student doing the required year of
training in a congregation. From the synod's leadership there was
resounding silence: nothing to offer me, and no communication at
all as I waited in Wilmington. I felt bitter and bereft, discarded by
the church I had been so eager to serve. I had expected to have
at least fifteen years in active ministry; now, it seemed that it was
over after just half of that. After a year and a half, I retired.

I had come to some kind of peace with it, accepting that my ministry as a pastor had ended. Then, a few months later, I was invited to serve as interim pastor at Fellowship Divine—the very congregation I had left in tears some twenty years before, and then returned to for my internship year. They'd had a painful ending with their pastor of many years, and now they were eager to come to terms with their history and move toward new life. They were concerned about recent losses in membership and participation, worried about money—the near-universal plaints of congregations—and yet privileged by comparison to most. I felt energized by their determination and readiness; in turn, they embraced me and were eager to work together.

When I was diagnosed with breast cancer a few months into the interim, they supported me through chemo and radiation with meals, cards, and prayers; most of all, even as they cared for me, they let me be their pastor. So they called on me, let me care for them, and sometimes challenged me. At Fellowship Divine we shared the powerful synergy of mutual flourishing, and even as I was grateful for their energy and openness, I also came to see that they had more in common with the Saints than I had imagined. Most of us cling to the churches we have known and loved; most of us fear change, even when we know that death is necessary for resurrection. And it's a hard time to be church. Maybe it always is.

When I'd finished my ministry there, I served at another local congregation for a short interim as they awaited their new pastor—again an opportunity to experience life together in a moment of transition.

These days, I am living out my call as a mentor and colleague to other rostered ministers. I serve in our synod as a convener of two ministeriums, colleague groups in which we plan shared ministries, study and discuss the Sunday readings to prepare for preaching, pray for one another, and hold one another up in the pain and joy of life together. Finally, though I have been writing for many years, writing this book has emboldened me to claim writing as my primary vocation.

It seems God is not done with me yet. Thanks be to God.

# ACKNOWLEDGMENTS

The Collegeville Institute of St. John's University nurtured this project from its inception and sustained me with the gift of Benedictine hospitality. I first imagined *Loving and Leaving a Church* as a book in 2010, thanks to Richard Lischer's searching and thoughtful seminar on memoir. In two return visits to Collegeville, I benefited from the companionship of other writers and the astute readings of Michael McGregor, gifted writer and coach extraordinaire. I am also indebted to the Collegeville Institute for friendships and writing partnerships that have shaped my work and enriched my life. When we met at a Collegeville writing retreat in 2012, Ruth Everhart invited me to join her writing group in northern Virginia; for their good advice and good company, many thanks to Ruth and MaryAnn McKibben Dana, Elizabeth Hagan, Leslie Klingensmith, and Martha Spong. In 2016 I returned to Collegeville and met Jane Willan, my writing partner. Our biweekly exchange of drafts enabled me to complete this book, and the parallel adventures of Jane's fictional detective enlivened that process.

The "Old Girls," my academic colleagues and longtime friends, accompanied me along the way from my ordination to my leave-taking, with dinners and sleepovers at the manse in between. They heard and read earlier versions of these stories. Thanks to Dina Copelman, Devon Hodges, Lorna Irvine, Rosemary Jann, Deborah Kaplan, Eileen Sypher, and Ellen Todd.

Clergy colleagues shared with me the joys and sorrows of our calling. Marda Messick shepherded me through seminary, became a weekly partner in sermon exchanges, called and visited as I undertook my ministry. I am also thankful for the collegiality and friendship of Michael Dubsky, Bill Gohl, Vicki Hamel, Laura Lincoln, Wendy Moen, Neil O'Farrell, John Sabatelli, Thomas R. Swears, and Lowell Thompson.

Several dear friends read the complete manuscript and provided helpful responses. I am deeply grateful for the generosity and encouragement of Cathy Loeb, Marda Messick, Christina Simmons, Eileen Sypher, Bruce Tucker, and John Yrchik.

My deep gratitude for Joanie Nicaise, who knows why.

Zofia Burr and Gary Kulik read the manuscript; and more, they lived its stories with me. I first knew Zofia as a colleague in the English department. She stayed close through my early discernment, seminary years, and ministry at Saints and Sinners. I thank God for the blessing of deep friendship. Gary Kulik was as shocked as I was when I said that I might want to leave academe for ministry—and responded on the spot with unconditional support. He encouraged me to follow my restless heart out of the university, and to take up and then let go of the ministry at Saints and Sinners. I thank God for the gift of marriage.

Finally, I am grateful to the people of Saints and Sinners. You called me "pastor," and among you I became one.